Howard Clinebell, PhD

Counseling for Spiritually Empowered Wholeness: A Hope-Centered Approach

Pre-publication REVIEWS, COMMENTARIES, EVALUATIONS . . .

"**O**nce again Dr. Clinebell elucidates his growth or wholeness approach toward helping. Since the 1970s, he has introduced tens of thousands of people to a way of caring for others that is based not upon pathology, but upon perceiving people as capable of growth, change, and creativity. Few people within or outside the field of pastoral care have done as much to advance this nonpathological approach to helping.

Clinebell sets out specific ways in which people can go about change in the many areas of their lives. In addition, he speaks to the reader as if she or he is also able to change. He writes with a growth perspective."

Howard W. Stone
Professor, Pastoral Theology and Pastoral Counseling, Brite Divinity School, Texas Christian University

" I am proud that my mentor in pastoral counseling has done it again with the publication of *Counseling for Spiritually Empowered Wholeness*. The author has the unique gift of looking realistically and soberly at the social evils on this planet, and the personal entrapments of individuals, couples, and families, and finding the creative psychological and spiritual resources and perspectives to help us transform those enslaving realities by liberating and growth-producing approaches.

Clinebell is the quintessential spokesperson for the empowerment of persons to grow their lives in creative ways, and to transform the world in ethical and just ways for everyone, regardless of gender, race, nationality, age, etc. Clinebell offers his finest ideas for a holistic, optimistic, and spiritually oriented [approach to] counseling."

Merle R. Jordan, ThD
*Albert V. Danielsen Professor
of Pastoral Psychology,
Boston University School of Theology*

" A future thinker in the pastoral care movement, Dr. Clinebell has long held a paradigm that sets pastoral care apart from psychotherapy, for pastoral care is oriented toward wholeness, not pathology. It is exactly what the church and we pastors should be about! This work provides a model that is learnable by seminary students and doable in the local church.

Formerly *Growth Counseling*, this work has been missed. It returns with a more descriptive table of contents, but retains its expansive view of wholeness, needed now more than ever. Excellent as a text for pastoral care courses, this revised work is also useful as continuing education for clergy who want to rethink their approach to ministry."

Carolyn J. Bohler, PhD
*Emma Sanborn Tousant Professor
of Theology and Counseling,
United Theological Seminary,
Dayton, Ohio*

More pre-publication
REVIEWS, COMMENTARIES, EVALUATIONS . . .

"**C**linebell has delineated a helpful framework for depiction and illustration of the seven ways of renewing ourselves and sparking others' potential on the journey called 'growthing.' The seven areas of growthful living simply resound with common sense. In each area he describes the dynamics of enriching and deepening our relationships of self to self to neighbor to spirit.

Dr. Clinebell does not minimize nor trivialize individual pathology or social evil. Still, he is less concerned with naming and blaming the origins of the vast growth-limiting structures, or even heralding one cause over another, than he is in pointing out the directions where healing, growth, and revitalization can take place.

This necessarily includes working to challenge and change the institutions and organizations of our community that diminish personhood and stifle community growth as a whole. For therapists this means understanding and addressing the role of personal and interpersonal power as inextricably linked with economic and political power. Wholeness counseling is growth counseling revisited and revitalized.

Professionals and laypeople alike will find this a strong theoretical and practical book integrating issues of self/neighbor/society/biosphere/spirit informing counseling in the increasingly complex networks in which we live."

Gail Unterberger, PhD
Assistant Professor of Pastoral Care and Counseling,
Wesley Theological Seminary,
Washington, DC

❧

"**F**or the past 25 years, Howard Clinebell has elegantly modeled the maturation process for me. His writings, and his life, prove his thesis that holistic wellness is realizable and worth its price.

In this volume, Clinebell effectively updates, synthesizes, and personalizes his impressive body of work. The book is especially timely in light of our growing awareness of the limitations of medicine's powers coupled with increased willingness to accept personal responsibility for one's own well-being. Bravo!"

John R. Landgraf, PhD
Executive Director,
Samaritan Counseling Center,
Palo Alto, California

The Haworth Pastoral Press
An Imprint of The Haworth Press, Inc.

Counseling for Spiritually Empowered Wholeness
A Hope-Centered Approach

The Haworth Pastoral Press
Religion , Ministry & Pastoral Care
William M. Clements, PhD
Senior Editor

New, Recent, and Forthcoming Titles:

Growing Up: Pastoral Nurture for the Later Years by Thomas B. Robb

Religion and Family: When God Helps by Laurel Arthur Burton

Victims of Dementia: Services, Support, and Care by Wm. Michael Clemmer

Horrific Traumata: A Pastoral Response to the Post-Traumatic Stress Disorder by N. Duncan Sinclair

Aging and God: Spiritual Pathways to Mental Health in Midlife and Later Years by Harold G. Koenig

Counseling for Spiritually Empowered Wholeness: A Hope-Centered Approach by Howard Clinebell

Shame: A Faith Perspective by Robert H. Albers

Dealing with Depression: Five Pastoral Interventions by Richard Dayringer

Counseling for Spiritually Empowered Wholeness
A Hope-Centered Approach

(originally published as *Growth Counseling*)

Howard Clinebell, PhD

The Haworth Pastoral Press
An Imprint of The Haworth Press, Inc.
New York • London

Published by

The Haworth Pastoral Press, an imprint of The Haworth Press, Inc., 10 Alice Street, Binghamton, NY 13904-1580

Originally published as *Growth Counseling: Hope-Centered Methods of Actualizing Human Wholeness* by Abingdon Press, copyright © 1979.

Scripture quotations unless otherwise noted are from the Revised Standard Version of the Bible, copyrighted 1946, 1952, © 1971, 1973, by the Division of Christian Education of the National Council of the Churches of Christ in the U.S.A. and used by permission.

Scripture quotations noted NEB are from The New English Bible. © the Delegates of the Oxford University Press and the Syndics of the Cambridge University Press 1961, 1970. Reprinted by permission.

Scripture quotations noted Phillips are from The New Testament in Modern English, copyright © J. B. Phillips 1958, 1960, 1972.

The lines of verse at the beginning of this volume are reprinted from the poem entitled "The Invocation to Kali" from A GRAIN OF MUSTARD SEED, POEMS BY MAY SARTON, copyright © 1971 by May Sarton. Reprinted with permission of W. W. Norton & Co., Inc., New York, New York.

Printed on partially recycled paper.

Library of Congress Cataloging-in-Publication Data

Clinebell, Howard John, 1922-
    Counseling for spiritually empowered wholeness: a hope-centered approach / Howard Clinebell.—[New ed.]
        p. cm.
    Includes bibliographical references and index.
    ISBN 1-56024-903-X (alk. paper).
    1. Pastoral counseling. 2. Self-actualization (Psychology) I. Title.
BV4012.2.C5325   1994
253.5—dc20   94-30384
                                                                              CIP

Help us to be the always hopeful
Gardeners of the Spirit
Who know that without darkness
Nothing comes to birth
As without light
Nothing flowers.

–May Sarton

ABOUT THE AUTHOR

Howard Clinebell, PhD, is Professor Emeritus of Pastoral Psychology and Counseling at The School of Theology at Claremont, California. He is widely recognized for his expertise in pastoral psychology, counseling, comparative psychotherapies, marriage and family enrichment and counseling, health and human well-being, and counseling alcoholics and their families. Dr. Clinebell has edited more than 25 books and written 14, some of which have been translated into eight different languages. A licensed marriage, child, and family counselor, he has led workshops or taught on topics discussed in this book in over 30 countries. Dr. Clinebell is the founder and former clinical director of both the Institute for Religion and Wholeness, and the Pastoral Counseling and Growth Center in Claremont, California. He is also a founder of the International Pastoral Care Network for Social Responsibility.

CONTENTS

Preface

SOME PERSONAL REFLECTIONS ABOUT THIS NEW EDITION

I am pleased that The Haworth Press has republished this book and that you are reading it. When I encounter a book, I find myself wondering about the person whose mind and life I touch in its pages. Why did that person choose to invest the irreplaceable segment of her or his life that was required to create it? What hopes and struggles, frustrations and dreams were the raw material out of which the book was generated? On the hunch that you might have a similar curiosity, here are some personal reflections about the new edition of this book.

My original reason for writing this book was to offer an introductory understanding of an empowering spiritual approach to counseling, therapy, and education about which I was excited, an approach which had developed in my professional practice over some two decades. In succinct form the book presented the heart of the approach called "growth counseling." (This was the original title. I now use "growth counseling" and "wholeness counseling" interchangeably.) The heart of this wholeness approach is seeing human beings through the *growth-hope-empowerment-spirituality perspective*. In my experience, this way of perceiving people is the most effective approach for awakening creative change in them. It's a way of inviting them to move into a new future by discovering their underdeveloped inner strengths and special gifts as unique human beings of irreducible value.

When considering doing a fresh edition, I chose not to rewrite the original radically, but to do only minor revisions and updating. Why? Because subsequent experiences had confirmed the core ideas of the book. In fact, my enthusiasm for the central thrusts of this approach has increased as I have been touched repeatedly by witnessing the miracle of people growing in unexpected ways, in one or often several dimensions of their turbulent lives.

On a personal level, during the years since the original edition, I have experienced a plethora of challenges, losses, and crises. Many of these have been related to normal losses associated with moving beyond life's mid-point. Others have stemmed from unexpected rough places on the road. I am thankful that these dark passages have been interspersed with many times of sunshine on the journey. In the midst of all this, I have applied the growth-hope approach to working with many others coping with difficult problems, but also seeking to discover and develop their many unused gifts. In this process of testing the ideas in my life and work, the central themes of this book–*growth and empowerment,* together with *hope* and *healthy spirituality*–have become increasingly validated as well as crucial. They are now essential resources in my professional life as a pastoral counselor, psychotherapist, and teacher, as well as in my personal life with my family and close friends.

It is gratifying that the earlier edition of this book has proved to be useful to persons in secular as well as religious professions, to lay counselors as well as professionals. Whatever your professional identity and work setting, I trust that this edition will prove to be useful in making your work with people more healing and growth-producing, and your organization more effective as a human wholeness center. If your work is in a congregation, school, or counseling-psychotherapy agency, I trust that you will be challenged to use the growth-hope-empowerment-spirituality principles in the educational as well as the healing dimensions of the program there.

If you are a clergyperson, I hope you will feel affirmed in your special expertise as a professional trained to facilitate spiritual wholeness. The approach described in these pages is rooted in the century-spanning healing and wholeness insights of the Christian and Jewish traditions. It also draws on other spiritual traditions. All these heritages include some time-tested understandings of brokenness and healing, despair and hope, alienation and reconciliation, guilt and forgiveness, tragedy and joy, trappedness and liberation, death and rebirth. My expectation is that this book, with its introductory spelling out of some of these spiritual insights, will make them more readily available to counselors, therapists, and teachers in all the people-growthing professions.

Although this book is targeted at counseling and teaching professionals, it is clear that many of the wholeness principles described are equally useful in other caring relationships–between friends, lovers, marriage partners (who may also be friends and lovers), and within families.

Wholeness counseling-therapy is explicitly eclectic in that it draws on a variety of psychotherapeutic and educational sources. It is an *integrated* eclecticism, the aim of which is to provide a unifying conceptual framework within which any professional or lay growth-facilitator can bring together insights and methods from the wealth of therapeutic and educational orientations available today.

My initial training in counseling and psychotherapy (at the William A. White Institute of Psychiatry in New York City), including my personal training therapy, was psychodynamic (neo-Freudian and Sullivanian). It was essentially pathology-oriented, and focused on changing intra-psychic dynamics. I still value and use much that I learned, particularly in understanding the dynamics of deeply blocked growth (pathology). But my sense that the individualistic, pathological model was incomplete has increased through the years since. So, the boundaries of the healing-growthing arts have continued to become more inclusive for me.

This book's major thrust is, as you are already aware, not the only effective way to do counseling, therapy, and education. But it is the most effective way I have found. There are many valuable insights and tools for facilitating healing and growth in other approaches. When traditional therapies are viewed from the growth perspective, their valuable resources become more readily available. (*Contemporary Growth Therapies*, see bibliography, does precisely this.)

What I have written reflects my own biases, values, and life experiences, of course. It also reflects something of my passionate vision for a healthier, more whole future for the human family and the rest of the incredible biosphere. I hope what is in these pages may relate at some points to what is really important to you–*your life experiences and your guiding vision for the future!*

This book is an introduction to growth-oriented approaches to the helping arts. In case you are interested in more comprehensive discussions of any topic discussed briefly in these pages, you may wish to consult one or more of my other books listed in the annotated bibliography. For example, *Basic Types of Pastoral Care and Counseling* is an in-depth exploration of the basic issues found in this book. (I am pleased as well as a little surprised that it is the most widely used text on the topic in graduate theological seminaries in the U.S.A.) Some secular counselors and psychotherapists, aware of the crucial spiritual component in sickness, healing, and health, have reported that the book proved to be a useful resource in their settings.

Well Being, A Personal Plan for Exploring and Enriching the Seven Dimensions of Life–Mind, Body, Spirit, Love, Work, Play, Earth, sets forth in non-technical language the holistic, spiritually centered, growth approach to caring and counseling, presented here and amplified in *Basic Types*. It is a self-care workbook in non-professional language exploring the seven dimensions of life and health–mind, body, spirit, relationships, work, play, and society. It also has chapters on the healing power of humor, self-care by women and men, and the care of the earth as essential to holistic self-care. There is a video series and a leader's guide written to help clergy and lay leaders in congregation use the book as a text in wellness classes, retreats, and workshops.

Now a look at a few key terms. *Growth* refers to the life-long process of developing the unique gifts of each stage. *Wholeness* is a term referring to this growth journey. *Counseling* is the short-term process of enabling people to mobilize their resources to cope with crises, both accidental and developmental, and gain some fresh strengths thereby. *Therapy* is short for *psychotherapy*, the often longer-term process of enabling people to find healing of old psychic wounds which have blocked growth, and reconstruct their lives, to some degree, for living more fully and productively. *Growth work* and its synonym *potentializing* refer to the process by which persons actively further their own healing and becoming. *Education*, like therapy, is a process of facilitating growth work by relatively functional or healthy people.

This book will fulfill my hopes to the degree that it:

- helps you understand in a clear, functional way, the basic principles and methods of this approach to counseling, therapy, and education;
- enables you to experience the transforming impact of the *growth-hope-empowerment-spirituality perspective* as a way of seeing and relating to people, beginning with yourself;
- helps encourage you and those with whom you have the privilege of working to overcome inevitable resistances to growth and to develop the valuable new assets and possibilities of one's present life stage;
- stimulates you to develop your own type of wholeness-enabling counseling, therapy, and education, reflecting your unique personhood and gifts as a person;
- increases your awareness of how spiritual growth-toward-wholeness is a major source of the energy that motivates all growth and therefore is an essential part of your task as a counselor, therapist, or teacher in whatever setting.

Two suggestions for deriving the most from this book:

- *Keep a growth journal* to record insights and reflections as you read, and perhaps your plans for next steps on your personal and/or professional growth journey.
- *Try the experiential exercises* near the end of the chapters. They're designed to give you a taste of a variety of growth-facilitating methods.

Years ago I had a session with Fritz Kunkel, a creative therapist whose books I had enjoyed, seeking guidance about my plans for graduate training in therapy. Still in a youthful yearning for heroes, I took one of Kunkel's books along hoping for his autograph. On the flyleaf he wrote these brief words: *"Good luck on the journey down and up."* Only in retrospect, after many years, could I grasp the full significance of what he had written. My hope is that encountering some of these ideas in this book may challenge and encourage you with hope on your growth journey–which I suspect will go down and up several times.

Chapter 1

The Goals of Wholeness
or Growth Counseling

Humankind will survive only through the commitment and involvement of individuals in their own and others' growth and development as human beings. This means development of loving and caring relationships in which all members are as committed to the growth and happiness of others as they are to their own. Through commitment to personal growth individual human beings will also make their contribution to the growth and development–the evolution–of the whole species to become all that humankind can and is meant to be.

> –Elisabeth Kübler-Ross, *Death: The Final Stage of Growth* (Englewood Cliffs, NJ: Prentice-Hall, 1975), p. 165.

Several years ago, while resting on the beach after snorkeling in Hawaii, I noticed a man walking along slowly, holding an electronic gadget just above the sand. I struck up a conversation with him and discovered that his gadget was a metal detector, an "electronic treasure-finder." He was using it to search for coins, wristwatches, and other valuable objects lost in the sand.

This "treasure-finder" struck me as a useful though imperfect image for depicting what effective growth-centered counselors, therapists, and teachers do. Our goal is to put treasure-finders into the hands of the persons with whom we work. Our purpose is to equip them to find their own buried treasures, the riches waiting to be developed in their inner lives and relationships.

Wholeness counseling is a spiritually empowered approach to the healing and helping processes that defines the goal as facilitating the maximum development of a person's potentialities, at each life stage, in ways that contribute to the growth of others as well, and to the development of a society in which all persons will have an opportunity to use their full potentialities. Growth Counseling aims at helping people achieve liberation from their prisons of unlived life, unused assets, and wasted strengths. The counselor or therapist is a *liberator,* an enabler of a process by which people free themselves to live life more fully and significantly. Through this freeing experience people discover that happiness is a by-product of actualizing their constructive potentials. Mental-physical-spiritual-relational health is the continuing movement toward living life more fully, joyfully, and productively. Wholeness is a growth journey, not the arrival at a fixed goal.

Human life is precious, much too precious to waste. To live at only a fraction of our potential aliveness and creativity is to waste much of our most valuable asset–life itself. Most of us sell ourselves short. We live by impoverished views of what is "normal" and "healthy." We tend to see health as the *absence* of gross dysfunction rather than the *presence* of a full, rich quality of consciousness, creativity, and relationships. Most of us are only dimly aware of our own capacities. We limit our options and truncate our growth by the illusion that our drab existence is all that is possible for us. We miss many of the satisfactions of participating more fully in the creative processes of living and helping to heal our world.

Wholeness Counseling sees people as possessing a wealth of unlived life. Evidence from the human sciences suggests that most of us "normal" people probably use no more than 15 to 25 percent of our potential intelligence and creativity, of our capacities for living more zestfully and effectively and for living in ways that enhance society.[1] Those whose growth is deeply blocked (usually described as mentally and emotionally ill) use even a smaller fraction of their gifts.

Darkness is the absence of light, but light is more than the absence of darkness. Light is the *presence* of energy moving at certain frequencies. Similarly, Wholeness Counseling sees health as much more than the absence of gross physical, emotional, interpersonal, or spiritual illness. Health is the presence of positive, developing wholeness. It is the ongoing process of fulfilling one's potentialities as they emerge and change in each life stage. Health, or better, wholeness is one's unique lifelong journey of growth.

The good news is that we *can* become more than we have hoped. It *is* possible to develop more growthful relationships with ourselves, others, nature, and God. Within such relationships we can gradually discover and develop many of our unused strengths. Effective counseling, education, and psychotherapy utilize growthful relationships to enable people to do their growth work. The goal of these helping arts is liberation–*from* whatever is diminishing growth, liberation *to* increased competence, hope and joy, and liberation *for* the well-being of society.

THE SEVEN DIMENSIONS OF GROWTH

It is important for the growth-oriented counselor or therapist to have a clear understanding of the seven interdependent dimensions within which growth can occur: *in our minds and in our bodies*, in our relationships *with other people, in our work and play*, with the *biosphere*, with the *institutions* that sustain us, and in the *spiritual dimension* of our lives. Growth in any of these dimensions stimulates and supports growth in the others. Diminished growth in one area retards growth in the others. The wholeness-oriented counselor seeks to help a person maximize and balance growth in all six facets. Fresh growth usually begins in one's inner life or one's relationships, though it may begin in other dimensions. Wherever it begins, growth will tend to spread to the other facets.

1. Inner Growth: Enlivening One's Mind

The first dimension of our growth involves developing our many-faceted personality resources including our intellectual capacities. What are some directions of this inner growth? Growing persons are moving toward increasing acceptance of and openness to themselves and others; growing awareness of and respect for reality; increasing self-support and self-esteem; relationships of creative interdependency; growing capacity to give and receive love; increasing intellectual competence and creativity; greater freshness of perception and richness of feelings (both joy and pain); a more aware, autonomous, and caring value system; a growing sense of affinity with the natural world and with humankind; a widening openness to newness and change; an increasing sense of at-home-ness in the universe; a greater frequency of moments of transcendence; a growing relationship with a loving higher Power; increasing androgynous wholeness; a growing aliveness and celebration of the good gift of life; an increasing playfulness and creativity, in spite of the losses in life; and a growing enjoyment of living in one's present experience, enriched by the experiences of one's past and by the sense of a hopeful future.[2]

By *androgynous wholeness* I mean a balanced development of one's vulnerable, nurturing, feelingful side (inaccurately labeled the "feminine" side of the personality by Carl Jung) and one's rational, assertive, analytic side (inaccurately labeled the "masculine" side). Most of us neglect developing fully one of these two sides of our personalities. Wholeness Counseling encourages people to nurture and integrate both sides, recognizing that they are complementary, equally valuable aspects of our full humanity as women or men.

The unused capacities of the human mind to learn, to think, and to create are enormous! On the basis of research in Russia, Ivan Yefremov declares, "If we were able to force our brain to work at only half its capacity, we could, without any difficulty whatever, learn forty languages, memorize a large . . . encyclopedia from cover to cover, and complete the required courses of dozens of colleges."[3] Few of us develop more than a small fraction of our capacity for intellectual competence and creativity. Lifelong, easily available, educational-growth opportunities in schools, churches, industries, social agencies, and clubs are needed to help us learn to develop and enjoy our unfolding intellectual assets.

Enriching our consciousness, the center from which we relate to other people and to the world, is crucial to enriching all other dimensions. I find that when my inner space feels dull and barren, I have little to give in my relationships. But when my inner life is lively and well nurtured my relationships improve dramatically. The enrichment of our consciousness involves becoming more alive and aware and more affirming of ourselves. Most of us need to discover that our real self is more lovable and capable, as well as more earthy and sometimes more obnoxious, than are the masks we wear to impress others and hide from ourselves. We need to learn how to value and care for ourselves, to enrich our "centers" in order to make them safe, strong, renewing places to be. We need to relate to other people and to the world out of this center, out of an inner wholeness in which our weaknesses and imperfections are accepted and transcended. All this is easier said than done. But it *is* possible! We can make our inner space a more lively place to be at home with ourselves.

Each person's coming alive to herself or himself is as unique as that person's fingerprints. I share the following experience of inner renewal because it's one I know from the inside. In a ten-day Gestalt Therapy workshop, I struggled ineffectively for the first nine days to solve a long list of reality problems and hang-ups and to be more transparent and *present* in my relationships with other group members. In spite of my painful struggles, my inner heaviness and self-despair increased. The night before the last day of the workshop, I went to bed in a mood of defeat, convinced that I was hopelessly trapped in professional rigidity reinforced by middle age. I felt myself to be in a no-exit space.

During the night I had what I was sure was a "highly significant" dream. I went to the workshop session *determined* to work through the dream and achieve release from my feelings of entrapment. I began to describe the dream in the present tense (in good Gestalt Therapy fashion) but in a heavy detached tone. As I went on with my report about the dream, I suddenly saw that the therapist had put a small, colorful pillow on his head and was clowning with his eyes and face. This triggered a rapid series of feelings in me. I moved from surprise and anger at his apparent rejection of my "important" dream to an awareness of the humorous absurdity of what I was doing–making a federal case of everything including my dream. We were sitting on the floor, and as this awareness dawned, I collapsed on the floor in spasms of spontaneous laughter, laughter coming from my center. My playful inner child (who had been the most neglected part of my inner life) was released. He celebrated with gales of laughter. As my outward laughter gradually subsided, my inner laughter continued. I became aware of an inner lightness, of bouncy, dancing feelings that I had not experienced to that degree in years. I sensed that my intense drive to achieve liberation by using the dream and the whole workshop "properly" was precisely what was blocking my liberation! The reality problems and inner goals that were on my long "agenda," no longer seemed urgent. They were no longer barriers that I had to surmount before I could allow myself to feel alive. I had the power to choose to be alive and free in that moment! I became aware that if I wait until I resolve all my hang-ups and solve all my mid-year problems, I'll never get around to enjoying being alive! I can experience the joy and pain of being aware in the present moment (and only in this moment). That was and is, at this moment as I write, a freeing awareness.

I continued in the workshop session to chuckle inwardly about my absurd self-deadening. My sense of aliveness came to focus in an image. I could see and feel a tumbling, sunlit mountain stream within me. It was like a stream I remember hiking along during a backpack trip with our sons in the high Sierras. The stream in me seemed to dance with abandon as it frolicked down its rocky course. Perhaps the rocks symbolized my continuing hang-ups and problems. It was the movement over those rocks in the stream bed that produced the dancing of the water. I knew then that that mountain stream is a part of me, a precious part to which I can return in my inner awareness.

In the workshop group I felt open and in touch with others in a way that was light and new. A short time later, I received a phone call telling me that a dear friend of my wife's family had died. My tears flowed more spontaneously than ever before in my adult life. Surprisingly, the sense of inner joy was still there. Somehow the joy and sorrow were strangely and closely linked. At the end of the workshop we said good-bye, not with words, but by moving joyously to lively music with a strong beat. I surprised myself with my freedom to enjoy moving spontaneously with others to a type of music I had not liked before that experience.

In the months since that experience, my awareness of the stream has come and gone and come again. A few days after the workshop, I was walking alone by the ocean. The dawning sun was sparkling on the surf. A line of a hymn I had enjoyed at a church youth camp came back to me: "Like your dancing waves in sunlight, make me glad and free." I realized that my recent awakening was something like a transforming religious experience at that camp some thirty-five years ago. As I walked on the deserted beach, I came upon a solitary egret fishing in the surf for its breakfast. We communicated nonverbally for a few minutes. Then the bird took off and soared in a gentle arc to the right over the water and back to the beach. I felt my spirit soaring with that egret, free as a bird. I experienced the lightness and lift of new aliveness and hope.

I find that I can return to the laughing, playful child, the dancing mountain stream, the sparkling ocean waves, the soaring egret within me. Often, in my preoccupation with *doing* and with *proving myself*, I lose touch with this liberating inner experience. It seems utterly lost. I feel sad, knowing that I have slipped back into the heaviness of my work addiction. But, on other occasions, I'm able to recover the inner aliveness. I do this in various ways–by moving to music (actual music or in my mind), by meditating and opening myself to the flow of life, by breathing more fully, or simply by chuckling inwardly at myself.

When I am in touch with my inner flow, my close relationships are more open and more satisfying. Writing and counseling and teaching are freer, more energizing experiences. In contrast to the many times I push myself to produce and do well, these activities are more productive and satisfying when I'm in touch with the inner stream of energy. It is clear that the inner stream of creativity is there potentially in all of us!

The inner liberation I experienced in that workshop was a gift, like grace. But how painful it was to become open enough to receive the gift. The nine days of struggle felt like a descent into hell. That descent was necessary to crack my shell of *doing* and open me to receive the gift of *being*. For me as a life-long workaholic, the healing-growthing gift came through laughter. My playful inner child was what broke through my inner closedness and let new life flow. The familiar words in the New Testament now have new meaning for me: "Unless you become like a little child." I hope that my sharing of this experience brings back warm recollections of similar moments of enlivening in your life.

2. Inner Growth: Revitalizing One's Body

The second dimension of growth involves revitalizing one's body by increasing awareness and learning to enjoy mind-body wholeness. Jerry, a "successful" graduate student, put it well in a creative singlehood group: "I've been head-tripping for a long time and collecting a lot of goodies by it from the academic world. But I've felt like my body, my guts and heart and genitals, weren't really 'me.' I've *used* them like they're not really vital parts of me that I love and care about. My body has been protesting in all kinds of ways, but I've been ignoring the message!" He went on to describe his new awareness and positive feelings about his body. He concluded, "I can be the alive person I want to be only if I'm an alive body!"

By concentrating almost exclusively on enhancing our psyches, most traditional psychotherapies have perpetuated and even increased that alienation from our bodies which has contributed to the impoverishment of our psyches. Drawing on the neo-Reichian body therapies and the exciting insights from biofeedback about mind-body complementarity, Wholeness Counseling aims at being a whole-person somato-therapy as well as a psychotherapy.

Alienation from our bodies is a major cause of nonpotentializing particularly among us middle-class people. We middle-class males tend to overvalue our intellects and consider our feelings and our bodies alien and inferior. Our bodies are experienced as things to be used, not really our selves. Consequently we cut ourselves off from experiencing the full spectrum of our feelings and our senses. Food is gulped compulsively and hardly tasted or enjoyed. Sex becomes mechanical and rushed rather than lusty, sensual, and savored in a relaxed, flowing way. We criticize and reject our bodies. We punish them by neglecting health-giving exercise, good nutrition, recreation, and rest.

Many middle-class females are alienated from their bodies but in another way. They also experience their bodies as things, as sex objects to be valued only as they are "attractive to men"–attractiveness being defined by the superficial criteria of Madison Avenue and Hollywood. Thus, both men and women become hypersensitive about the inevitable imperfections of their bodies. We work frantically to make them appear right according to our culture's superficial standards of youthful attractiveness. Our alienation from our bodies has been increased by negative views of the body and of sex in some Christian theologies. Awakening, revitalizing, and affirming our bodies is, for many of us, an essential part of the growth work by which we can move toward greater wholeness.

Over the years I have pushed and used my body like a machine. This chronic, self-imposed stress has contributed to various health problems and to a diminished sense of physical well-being. When I regress into my work addiction, I tend to breathe shallowly and anesthetize my body awareness. But I know that I *can* affirm and enjoy my body if I choose. At this moment, as I work on this paragraph, I am aware of how good it feels to breathe deeply and to be in touch with my body. When I work in a flowing, full-body way, the tension and fatigue do not build up so quickly in me. When pressures mount within me, I can choose to interrupt them with "pleasure breaks"–moving freely for a few moments to my own inner rhythms or taking a ten-minute minivacation to stretch and breathe and relax in the sun. Taking regular body-pleasure breaks stimulates my mental processes, raises my energy level, and helps make work more productive and satisfying.

3. Renewing Our Relationships

The third major dimension of our growth involves strengthening and enriching our intimate relationships. Enhancing one's consciousness and body awareness is an appropriate place to start, but not to stop, in personal growth work. Growth toward mind-body wholeness feeds and is fed by growth toward interpersonal wholeness. Two persons who are growing in mind-body aliveness are able to relate in ways that nurture their mutual growth as well as their love.

A loving relationship is one in which the persons are committed both to their own and to each other's growth. If I really care about a person, I care intensely about the things that enable her or him to grow. To the degree that I care, I will do everything I can to encourage and nurture that person's continuing growth. Love flowers fully only in a bond of mutual growth!

When I get out of touch with my body or lose awareness of my center, my intimate relationships take on a detached, distant quality. When I feel alive and in touch with my body and am with someone who feels alive, there is warmth, spontaneity, and mutual flow in our interaction. It is in my closest relationships that I experience both the most painful regressions into old rigidities and the best moments of mutual openness, pleasuring, and excitement.

We human beings do not just *have* relationships. In a profound sense, we *are* our relationships. Our personalities are formed by the significant relationships of our childhood. We carry these relationships within us throughout our lives. For better or worse we are, as the Bible puts it, "members of each other." The *will-to-relate* is more powerful than the will-to-pleasure (emphasized by Sigmund Freud), the will-to-power (emphasized by Alfred Adler) or the will-to-meaning (emphasized by Viktor Frankl). This is because it is only in meaningful relationships that we can satisfy our human need for pleasure, power, and meaning or, for that matter, satisfy any other psychological needs. The quality of our ongoing relational support system and the quality of our inner lives enhance or diminish each other reciprocally.

Wholeness Counseling recognizes that the most important factor in determining the degree to which we continue to develop our potential through the years is the continuing growth of our significant relationships. Psychological research shows that in order to cope with crises and continue growing we must have some depth relationships in which mutual feeding of our heart hungers (our basic psychological needs) occurs regularly and dependably.[4] Research by social psychiatrist E. Mansell Pattison showed that "normal" persons have, on the average, twenty to thirty persons in their psychosocial network of meaningful relationships. "Neurotics" average only ten to twelve persons in their support system, and "psychotics" only four or five. The quality of these relational networks also contrasted sharply. Those in the normal group had open, reciprocal, largely positive, mutually helpful networks drawn from family, relatives, friends, and work-recreational associates. The neurotics had less interconnection with those within their support group which often included people who lived far away or who were dead. The psychotics were caught in small, rigid, mutually destructive and constrictive social networks.[5] The impoverishment of one's relational support system produces emotional malnutrition and diminished growth. For this reason, Wholeness Counseling is inherently relationship-oriented. It aims at enriching simultaneously one's inner being and one's significant, need-satisfying relationships. As D. H. Lawrence put the matter: "As we live, we are transmitters of life. And when we fail to transmit life, life fails to flow through us."[6]

There's rich potential in most close relationships waiting to be discovered and developed. Relationship-centered counseling approaches, such as conjoint couple counseling and family therapy, have opened exciting understandings of how the emotional climate of a marriage or a family can facilitate or frustrate the growth of *everyone* within that interpersonal system. Often the most effective as well as the most efficient way to help an individual whose growth is severely diminished is to help that person's whole family learn how to communicate more clearly, honestly, and caringly. When that occurs, all the family members are freer to grow. That family has become an environment that facilitates rather than frustrates growth work.

That an intimate social system is a psychological organism that either enables or blocks growth for all its members, has enormous implications for counseling, therapy, and preventive growth groups. A disturbed marriage, for example, is one in which there is a vicious cycle of self-other growth-blocking. Conversely, a healthy marriage is one in which the growth work of both partners is nurtured by their ways of relating. Systems therapies treat the impoverished marriage or family interaction, per se, as the target of creative change.

Marriage and family enrichment aims at making functional marriages and families more effective by teaching the members of these social systems communication skills that nurture mutual growth. It is an exciting moment when a couple discovers that they *can* intentionally strengthen their love for each other by growth-nourishing communication. To illustrate, the Intentional Relationship Method (which I have described in detail elsewhere) is an excellent communication tool that functional couples and families can use to enhance their mutual growth.[7] At the close of a marriage-enrichment retreat Sally and Joe, a couple in their early forties, wrote this evaluation of their experience in using this communication tool:

By telling each other what we appreciate about each other we became more aware of how much we have going *for* us in our relationship. That felt good! Then, by spelling out what we want and need from each other, we saw how we can make our love grow–by choosing to meet more of each other's wants and needs. Now we've made an action plan to meet each other's specific needs. We feel like we've stopped drifting and hoping things would get better in our marriage. Instead, we're planning to do the things we need to do to make it better!

This couple was learning the skills of building on their strengths in ways that enable each of them *and* their relationship to grow. During the retreat, they had enjoyed being part of a sharing group with three other couples. This group decided to continue meeting monthly after the retreat to encourage one another's continuing growth. Eventually they became a kind of self-chosen extended family, an ongoing caring group that undergirded continuing enrichment of their lives and their marriages.

4. Growth in Relating to the Biosphere

The fourth dimension of our growth is in our ecological awareness and caring. This involves deepening and enriching our relationship with the biosphere, the total natural environment upon which we, along with all living things, depend for the quality of our lives and for our very survival. Personal potentializing is deeply constricted by our alienation from nature. We treat the air, the soil, the plants, and the animals around us as if they were alien things to be exploited rather than companions on the planet to be respected, cared for, and enjoyed.

Many of us desperately need the renewal of body, mind, and spirit that can come from enjoying our organic relatedness with the natural world. Bruno Walter, the famous conductor, developed a partial paralysis of his right arm after the birth of his first child. When his paralyzed limb failed to respond to medical treatment, he sought Sigmund Freud's help. After a few sessions, Freud recommended that, instead of further psychoanalysis, he take a vacation in Sicily that would include extended periods of sitting on the beach in the warm sun. He did so, his paralysis disappeared, and he had no further trouble with his conducting arm during his long career.[8] His experience is a dramatic illustration of the healing potential in our relations with the natural world.

I enjoy sitting in my swimsuit on our deck while I read and reflect and meditate. Experiencing the caress of the sun on my skin (protected by sun block), letting myself flow with the pulsing vitality of the flowers and trees, drinking in the song of the birds, and the views of the blue Pacific—all these bring a healing awareness of oneness with the natural world. It is noteworthy that for a while after the Gestalt Therapy workshop, I found that the colors of the sky and the grass, the flowers and mountains, seemed much more vivid and alive.

The increasing ecological crisis on planet Earth probably won't be reversed until millions of us develop ecological awareness and caring, until we awaken to what Francis of Assisi knew when he spoke of communicating with "brother wind" and "sister birds." We will not stop our massive pollution of the fragile, life-supporting biosphere unless we learn to respect, love, and be nutured by it as a profound part of ourselves, which it truly is. Increasing that sense of deep affinity with the natural world which is a part of the spiritual heritage of many tribes of Native Americans should be one goal of growth-oriented counseling. One can move toward this goal by becoming aware that one is profoundly involved in the whole interdependent life process. In the ecosystem the quality of our lives and that of all other living things is intimately interdependent. Increasing this awareness involves developing a sense of communion with Mother Earth. From this can flow an ecological consciousness and conscience and a life-style marked by active caring about the whole earth and all living things. Developing an ecological consciousness and conscience is not an expression of sentimental nature mysticism, as some have claimed. It is becoming increasingly crucial for our very survival.

5. Growth in Work and Play Life

The fifth dimension of growth focuses on two interrelated aspects of everyone's wholeness—work and play. Many people's well being is hurt or enhanced by the quality of their work and/or their play. Doing work you like and at which you are competent has many rewards. These include the satisfactions of providing financially for yourself, other people, and causes you care about, and the awareness that you are doing something worthwhile with your time and talents. Conversely, being unemployed or under-employed, or trapped in a boring, repetitive job, or in high stress, invitation-to-burnout work, can diminish painfully your self-esteem and zest for life. One goal of wholeness counseling and therapy is to help people make their work as meaningful, fulfilling, and esteem-building as possible.

To contribute most to wholeness, our work needs to be balanced by constructive play. So much recreational time is not re-creating because it is spent in high-stress, exhausting activities. To laugh at yourself and with others regularly is an inexpensive and always-available stress reducer. It can be a vital gift you can give to the growth of our mind, body, spirit, and relationships. Laughter and appropriate playfulness at work can enhance our well being in the workplace. This time-tested wisdom is stated well in the Hebrew Bible: "A cheerful heart is good medicine, but a downcast spirit driest up the bones." (Proverbs 17:22) The personal anecdote of my unexpected breakthrough at the Gestalt Therapy workshop via spontaneous laughter illustrates the healing-growthing power of playfulness. The self-care plan people are encouraged to generate in wholeness counseling should include attention to enhancing playfulness and renewal breaks in their lives. (For a full discussion of work and play, see "Enhancing Well Being & Avoiding Burnout in Your Work" and "Using Laughter and Playfulness for Healing and Health" in Clinebell's *Well Being*, Chapters 6 and 7.)

6. Growth in Relation to Organizations and Institutions

The fifth dimension of growth involves enhancing our relation with and helping to improve those organizations and institutions that can sustain our growth. Growing individuals and relationships can flourish best only in a community and in a society whose groups and institutions support growth. Unfortunately, many of our institutions stymie rather than stimulate and support the growth work of persons. A school where education is essentially indoctrination rather than an adventure of the mind, blocks intellectual growth. Or a church or synagogue where rigid belief systems and authoritarian leaders stifle spiritual autonomy and creativity, starves rather than nourishes spiritual growth.

How can counseling and growth groups further human survival on a livable planet? Is Growth Counseling and *all* counseling and therapy, for that matter, merely the privatized luxury of middle-class people in affluent countries? If so, they are unethical luxuries on a planet where two-thirds of the world's peoples face the ravages of economic oppression, malnutrition, and overpopulation. To be ethical, the insights and methods of counseling and life enrichment work must be used as instruments for helping to liberate social structures and institutions. Somehow we must integrate a passion for social justice into all our counseling, therapy, and growth groups. Participants should, as a central dimension of their growth, be motivated and empowered to join with others in eliminating growth-stifling economic injustice, racism, sexism, ageism, militarism, and nationalism wherever they occur. Commitment to the growth perspective implies a commitment to overcoming all those oppressive laws and beliefs and practices in our institutions, communities, and nation-states that block human becoming on a massive scale. Unless we implement such a commitment, our efforts to liberate human growth on an individual basis through creative counseling and education are doomed to failure! Personal, relational, ecological, and institutional liberation should be seen as interdependent dimensions of the holistic process of creative change. Each level of change is needed to sustain the other levels.

Thus Wholeness Counseling aims at freeing and empowering people to become effective change agents in their community's institutions. This involves encouraging them to join with others in using their collective power to transform the growth-inhibiting practices of the organizations and institutions of which they are a part. In growth-action task groups, people can discover how to avoid giving their power away to authority figures and to authoritarian institutions. They can then collaborate with like-minded persons in using their collective influence and political power to change the law, customs, and institutional practices that diminish personhood. When oppressed people exercise their personal influence and political power intentionally in this way, they tend to grow. For example, when disadvantaged ghetto residents in Chicago participated together in social action to improve their economic situation, it was found that some persons experienced positive personality growth. The apathy flowing from hopelessness and the absence of a viable future were reduced and self-esteem enhanced by learning to use their collective power to improve things for themselves and their community.[9]

Wholeness Counseling, to be true to its vision, must sometimes be countercultural. It must refuse to settle for adjusting persons to growth-diminishing relationships, groups, or institutions. It must be counseling for economic and political, as well as personal and relational, liberation. The *long-range* goal toward which we must continually work is to help provide for everyone on planet Earth the opportunity for a quality of life that will enable them to develop their full potentialities. Feminist therapy and other radical therapies have provided useful tools for integrating a passion for personal growth and social change. (See Clinebell, *Contemporary Growth Therapies*.)

To help reduce institutional oppression, Wholeness Counseling must see that *power* (so often ignored in psychotherapy) is a central, inescapable issue in all counseling, therapy, and growth work. Power is the ability to cause or prevent change. Powerlessness— emotional, interpersonal, economic, political–damages self-esteem, cripples relationships, and truncates personal growth. Personal and interpersonal power are inextricably linked with economic and political power.[10] One important goal of Wholeness Counseling is to encourage people to claim their legitimate strengths as persons and to use that power constructively, that is, in ways that will maximize the growth opportunities of themselves and others. Rollo May points out that power used against others is *manipulative*, *exploitative*, or *competitive* power. In contrast, power for others is *nutrient* power, and power used cooperatively with others is *integrative* power.[11] The growth-oriented counselor-therapist-teacher seeks to help people learn how to increase and use their power in nutritive, integrative, growthful ways.

The Gandhi-King-Day principle is a valuable conceptual tool for the growth counselor. Mahatma Gandhi, Martin Luther King, Jr., and Dorothy Day embodied in their life-styles a dual commitment to personal-spiritual growth on the one hand and societal trans-formation on the other.[12] Let me illustrate how this principle can be used. A "grief group" in a small church met weekly for six sessions. The members experienced the mutual healing that comes from sharing their feelings of deep pain and loss. They gradually became a growth group as together they discovered that there *were* growth opportunities even in their losses. During the last of the weekly sessions they decided to continue meeting once a month to encourage one another's growth. They also decided to be available, under their pastor's leadership, to call on other bereaved persons in that congregation and community to offer listening, understanding, and caring. Thus they moved from being primarily a *mutual-help group* to also being a *growth group* and then to becoming an *outreach group* to other bereaved persons in their community. The next step by such a group, in implementing the Gandhi-King-Day principle, would be to move into institutional change by forming a funeral cooperative to reduce the exorbitant cost of funerals, for example, or working with other concerned groups to change exploitative funeral laws in their state.

Growth pursued for its own sake eventually becomes a dead-end street. Using one's growth to support the growth of others and to change growth-diminishing institutional practices becomes a stimulus for further personal growth. In the closing phase of marriage-enrichment retreats or groups, I encourage the couples to decide what they will do to support each other's continuing growth and to provide enrichment for other couples in their community. As a result of such a discussion, one couples' group decided to organize an annual marriage enrichment retreat for their church, attendance at which is strongly encouraged especially for recently married couples and couples planning to be married within the year. By means of an ongoing marriage enrichment program a minister in another church has trained twenty-four married couples to give caring support to young couples beginning marriage. Outreach through such channels is integral to continuing marital growth.

The most growth-limiting factor in the lives of many women is the way culturally programmed sex-role stereotypes and sexist institutional practices limit their options for the full use of their intelligence, creativity, and leadership potentials. All women, married or single, suffer diminished self-esteem because of the sexism of our society. But married women's options for the full use of their potentials are even more constricted. Research reported by Jessie Bernard and Judith Laws shows that marriage is oppressive to the full potentializing of women in our culture (and in most other cultures).[13] Single women are healthier both physically and psychologically than married women. In contrast, married men are generally healthier than single men, in our culture.

It is also clear that the full potentializing of most men is limited by sexism. Those of us who are white, middle-class males are "oppressed oppressors." Male-role stereotypes, and the "success" treadmill implicit in them, block our growth in subtle but destructive ways.[14] As a male, I have tended to allow oppressive cultural expectation for what it is to "be a man" to fuel my work addiction; to prevent my developing fully my soft, vulnerable, feelingful side; to limit my intimate involvement in the nurture of our children; and to make it difficult for me to nurture myself effectively. I continue to struggle to liberate myself from this culturally programmed self-oppression.

In both marriage counseling and enrichment it is crucial to help couples face the fact that marriage *can* be a rich experience of mutual growth. But it *will* be so only if they design their working agreement (their marriage covenant or contract) so that both parties have maximum and equal opportunities for education and other growth-stimulating experiences and for vocational roles that use their full potentialities. This usually means that child-rearing and homemaking will be shared and that women will have an equal opportunity to have fulfilling careers outside the home, if they choose. Marriage enrichment and marriage counseling that lack an emphasis on equal growth can help lock couples more tightly into narrow sex roles that actually are counterproductive to their enrichment and growth![15]

7. Spiritual Growth

The seventh dimension of personal growth work–*spiritual growth*–intersects the other six dimensions and is their unifying bond. Spiritual growth is at the heart of all human growth because it has to do with those things that most clearly define us as being distinctively human. Spiritual growth aims at the enhancement of our realistic hope, our meanings, our values, our inner freedom, our faith systems, our peak experiences, and our relationship with God. The meanings that give our lives purpose, the values that guide our choices, and the quality of our relationship with God, all influence in profound ways the other six dimensions—the quality of our consciousness and of our body awareness, the quality of our relationships with others, the biosphere, our work and play, and social institutions. *Salugenic*, or growth-nurturing, religion enriches all other dimensions of life. *Pathogenic*, or growth-blocking, religion diminishes all these dimensions.

A key to human flowering is an open, trustful, nourishing relatedness with the loving Spirit which is the source of all life, all healing, all growth. The development of a growing energizing relationship with this wellspring of our being is an essential goal of growth-oriented counseling. Chapters 4 and 5 will explore the nature of spiritual growth and methods for facilitating it.

GROWTH AS A UNIFIED PROCESS

Growth Counseling affirms the organic unity of these seven dimensions. They are interdependent facets of human growth. Unfortunately, our culture compartmentalizes these dimensions, dividing concern for them among different professions and institutions. This fact increases the importance of recovering an awareness of the unity of whole-person growth. It should be clear from the above discussion that there is no such thing as isolated "*self*-fulfillment" or "*self*-actualization." Genuine self-actualization always involves self-transcendence! Authentic self-fulfillment results from participating in a process of self-*other* fulfillment, self-*society*, and self-*environment* fulfillment.

It is important for the counselor to be aware that the potentialities of persons are not just within them but are in their *total situation*. All dimensions of their lives and their particular cultural and historical setting offer resources and limitations to their growth. For example, the growth options of people living in economically disadvantaged countries or in impoverished ghettoes in affluent countries are drastically curtailed by their social setting. The struggle to survive in the face of hunger, disease, and poverty limits the full use of inner resources that might flower in a more favorable environment. Furthermore, there are possibilities for potentializing that are unique to each historical period. Prehistoric cave persons probably had a range of innate intelligence comparable to ours, but the potential of any individual for discovering the theory of relativity was not present. That potential emerged through a millennia-spanning process of social change that eventually provided the historical context within which the genius of an Einstein could flower.[16]

The image of the treasure-finder with which I began this chapter has the limitations of seeming to suggest that one's potential is innate and fixed, like a buried treasure. In reality, human potentialities are "given" *only in part* by hereditary endowment and by family, cultural, and historical circumstances. Our growth options are continually evolving. Possibilities change as we choose to use or not use particular capacities. Each new life stage brings fresh possibilities and limitations. As our family and societal contexts change continually, growth options are closed and opened. Even persons with very limiting cultural or early-life circumstances can make constructive choices within those limitations, choices that increase their future options. *In the flow of one's life, today's choices limit or expand tomorrow's growth possibilities. A person's potential is a dynamic, developing, changing stream, not a fixed quantity to be uncovered.*

Most human beings possess a wide variety of capacities, a wealth of things they could learn to do well. But time and energy are limited in any one life. Thus, life is choice, and every choice is a cutting off of other choices. To illustrate, the countless hours I am choosing to use in writing this book will never be available for other things I may have the capacity to do and enjoy.

The crucial issue in human growth, then, is *choice.* Do those aspects of your potential that you are choosing to develop represent the things that are most important–to you, to the people you care about, to the society that needs your talents? How can you use the valuable, limited time remaining in your life so that you'll maximize your creativity, your fulfillment and enjoyment, *and* the significance of your life for others? Do the values that guide all your choices need revising? It's important for one's growth that constructive answers be found to these hard questions.

EXPERIENCING THE SEVEN DIMENSIONS OF GROWTH

The purpose of this exercise is to increase your awareness of some ways in which you can intentionally experience growth in the seven growth dimensions. You'll need a quiet place and at least twenty uninterrupted minutes to use this exercise fully; you can do it by yourself although it may be more meaningful if done with a friend or in a growth group. Read the following instructions until you come to the slash (/), then close your eyes while you do what has been suggested.

1. Before you sit down, hunch and wiggle your shoulders, and tense and release the muscles all over your body. Do this until you *feel* your whole body. / Now, sit in a chair or on the floor in a comfortable position with your lower spine in a vertical position. Close your eyes and experience your body. Be aware of how it feels–tension, pain, pleasure, heaviness, strength, energy–whatever you are now experiencing in different parts of your body. / Do whatever is necessary to enhance your experience of your body–for example, concentrate on your breathing, and let the tension flow out with each exhalation, and let renewing energy flow into the parts of your body that feel tired or heavy as you inhale. / Be aware of the pleasurable flow of energy revitalizing your body. Let yourself *be* in your body now for a few minutes. /

2. Keeping in touch with your body, picture your consciousness as a room within yourself, a place where you are alone in your awareness. / Look around the room. Be aware of its size, color, furnishings, temperature, and how you feel right now in the room of your consciousness. / Do whatever you need to do, in your imagination, to make your room more comfortable and enjoyable. If it feels cramped, push back the walls and ceiling and make it larger. Give your spirit more room to breathe. Do whatever you wish–redecorate, clear up the clutter, add a picture window, comfortable furniture, a fireplace, etc. It's your

room; so make it a good place to be. / Just enjoy your inner space now in a quiet, nurturing way. /

3. Keeping in touch with your body and your consciousness, think of the person you would most enjoy being with right now. Picture that person vividly. / Let yourself be close to her or him, relating in warm, loving ways. / Be aware of how your feelings have changed. / Picture other people joining you, being aware of how your experience changes as you relate closely with them. / If you're doing this exercise in a group, join hands with those on both sides, keeping your eyes closed to focus on what you're experiencing. / Be aware of the two people with whom you've joined hands–persons with a variety of feelings, hopes, joys, and pain, many of these like yours. Be aware of the other people holding hands around your group. See if you can feel your connectedness as members of one family, the human family, whatever your differences. / Let yourself experience the flow of energy from you and to you, around the circle. /

4. Staying in touch with your body, your inner consciousness, and other people, become aware of your wider environment–the air, the room, the light coming through the windows. / Enlarge your awareness to include the wider world outside the building–the wind and trees and plants and birds and people. Let yourself feel your connectedness to all living things. Let your body-mind experience being supported by the earth and nurtured by your intimate bond with the whole creation. Feel the flow of energy from you and to you in the web of living things. / Let yourself feel the interdependence of yourself with all living things in the biosphere. /

5. Staying aware of your body, your inner room, your relationships with people and with nature, form a mental picture of your workplace. / *Be* in that place now, being aware of how you really feel there. What parts of your experience there feel fulfilling and worthwhile? / What parts cause you to feel unappreciated and de-energized? / Move back and forth between these two parts, seeing if you can take some of the energy from the healthy part to heal the other part of your work experience. /

Now, in your imagination, let yourself have some fun for a

while. Be playful with a friend or lover. Have a good laugh, being aware of how you feel when your inner child plays. / How can you take some of the carefree lightness and joy into the other dimensions of your life? /

6. Think of other important social and political institutions that are an integral part of your life–the neighborhood, community, organizations, congregation, region of the country, nation, etc. / Get inside your relations to one of these institutions. What is its feeling climate? Is it nurturing or depleting, just or unjust, healing or toxic? / Be aware of your own responses to this climate. / What can you do to change the institution itself, to make it more supportive of growth in yourself and others? / Do the same, if you wish, with your other significant institutions. /

7. Keeping in touch with what you have experienced in all these dimensions of your life, become aware of the presence of God's Spirit, Source of all life and growth and healing. Tune in on the energy of that nurturing, renewing reality. / Feel the flow of spiritual energy through your body/mind, in your relationships, and in nature. / Think of persons who need healing and wholeness. Surround them, one by one, with this transforming energy. / Infuse the key institutions in your life with this power. / Be aware of the lift of experiencing the vertical dimension of your life. / Express your feelings in some way that seems appropriate for the gift of life and growth in all the dimensions of your being. / Finish the experience in whatever way you wish and then gently open your eyes. / Share whatever you learned in this exercise with someone you trust. /

I hope that you experienced the interrelatedness of all these dimensions of personal growth and some renewal of life energy in each of them. If you found this awareness exercise meaningful, I suggest that you repeat it regularly, being aware of how your experiences in using it change.

Chapter 2

The Working Principles
of Wholeness Counseling

It is as if Freud supplied to us the sick half of psychology and we must now fill it out with the healthy half. Perhaps this health psychology will give us more possibilities . . . for improving our lives and for making ourselves better people. Perhaps this will be more fruitful than asking "how to get *unsick*."

–Abraham H. Maslow, *Toward a Psychology of Being* (New York: Van Nostrand, 1968), p. 5.

Every approach to counseling and therapy has certain key ideas that are its conceptual tools. The purpose of this chapter is to spell out the essential working concepts of the growth-oriented counselor. Someone has said that nothing is so practical as a good theory. I agree. This chapter will set forth the basic theoretical tools of Wholeness Counseling.

POTENTIALIZING–AN ENERGIZING PERSPECTIVE

The aim of Wholeness Counseling is to facilitate and accelerate *potentializing*, the ongoing process of growth work by which people actualize their emerging capacities. Implicit in this concept is the conviction that most people have significant unused resources and the latent ability to develop these assets and strengths throughout their lives.

How does potentializing relate to the needs of contemporary Western cultures? There is evidence that potentializing is an idea whose time has come. The spirit of our period of history, its zeitgeist, gives this theme increasing relevance and power. There is a widespread search in our times for new ways of liberating the potentials of ordinary people. The increasing interest in growth-oriented therapies, in meditation and other ways of enriching consciousness; the proliferation of human growth programs; the widespread participation in marriage and family enrichment; the profound changes in the identity of women—these are but a few of the many indications of what may be the dawning of a human-growth renaissance. The human-liberation movements around the world, in both the developing and the technologically advanced countries, have a common motif: the passionate striving of oppressed peoples for a full opportunity to develop their potentials. All around the planet a social *revolution of becoming*—sometimes stormy, sometimes quiet—seems to be gathering momentum.

On this theme, Duane S. Elgin, a social-policy analyst at Stanford University's Research Institute, has declared that a new frontier has opened in America. This frontier involves the efforts to realize our individual and collective human potential on an unprecedented scale. Speaking of human consciousness, he writes: "Metaphorically, it is as though we live and love in a small, cramped, one-room house—thinking that this room is our house in its entirety. Yet, if we were only aware, we would find our house is a mansion of many different rooms."[1] A comparable frontier of potentializing is, in my experience, gradually opening up around the globe.

POTENTIALIZING IN ECOLOGICAL PERSPECTIVE

We human beings now have available a new way of viewing ourselves and our world. This perspective could help us learn how to survive together on a livable planet. Pause for a minute and recall those remarkable pictures of the earth taken from the moon by the cameras of the astronauts. Reexperience your feelings as these awesome scenes were projected *live* onto the television screen in your living room and in hundreds of thousands of living rooms around the globe. There it was, a small blue-green ball, moving through the frigid, oxygenless void of space, a precious oasis of life and growth! Hold this image in your mind and be aware of how fragile, limited, and interdependent the life-nurturing resources of our planetary space-capsule really are. Let yourself feel the full impact of this new perspective. Be aware that full potentializing will be possible for us as individuals, in the long run, only as it becomes available to the whole human family, and other living beings, with whom we are profoundly interdependent.

Duane Elgin holds that participation in the frontier of human growth requires commitment to two interdependent ethical principles. These must be *a human-wholeness ethic* which commits our energies to maximizing the growth of persons and *an ecological ethic* which motivates us to work to make the whole ecosystem a place of growth. I agree. To be viable, growth approaches to counseling, therapy, and education must involve a planetary perspective that produces a whole-earth conscience, an ecological consciousness and caring.

The whole-earth perspective brings the significance of the contemporary health renaissance into sharp focus and clarifies the immorality and idiocy of our greedy consumption-oriented life-styles. We have no right to rob future generations by squandering the earth's limited resources, leaving a depleted, polluted planet to our children. The absurdity of our destructive intergroup and international relations also becomes evident. We're like stupid astronauts fighting one another for more room and power and possessions inside our spaceship rather than cooperating so that all can survive and share fairly in our limited resources. Obviously there cannot be a good future for the human family unless we relinquish the seductive illusion of endless technological growth in the affluent countries, share the positive benefits of appropriate technology fairly with developing countries, and interrupt the population explosion around the planet. But it is also painfully clear that relinquishing our compulsive attachment to self-destructive forms of quantitative growth won't be easy. Such a transformation will occur only when we human beings in increasing numbers discover the more sustainable and ecologically viable forms of qualitative growth–personal, relational, and transpersonal-spiritual growth.

That destructive forms of growth are best interrupted by creative growth is illustrated by what has occurred in several developing countries around the world. The birthrate declined significantly when women in those cultures had increased opportunity to develop their economic, intellectual and leadership potentials. When they could use more of their potentials, they did not need to derive their major feelings of worth and power and meaning from having many children.

Unlike the growth of economic power and population, personal, interpersonal, and transpersonal-spiritual growth contributes to the growth of others. Your growth may make it easier for me to grow, and my growth may make it easier for you to grow, if together we create a mutually growth-nurturing relationship. (A close relationship like marriage may be deeply strained, of course, if the two persons grow in different directions or at radically different rates.) As we experience personal growth, we'll have the heightened energy, motivation, and caring to join with others to create more growth-enabling groups, institutions, and communities. The potential for personal growth, unlike economic and population growth, is unlimited.

THE GROWTH ÉLAN

In all living things there is an inherent striving toward fulfilling their possibilities. Every acorn has a "need" to become an oak. All human beings have a deep need and striving to develop their full, authentic personhood. This growth élan is the basic motivation and source of energy for all potentializing. All growth depends ultimately on this innate drive toward actualization. The effectiveness of any teacher, counselor, therapist, or parent depends on her or his ability to stimulate and cooperate with the growth drive in persons. The growth élan is there in every person who's still alive. It's a tender, persistent striving. Often, however, it is distorted, diminished, and deeply blocked. Counseling and therapy are ways of helping people liberate themselves from such diminished growth.

The growth process has been explored from a variety of educational and psychotherapeutic perspectives. The students of growth who have influenced my understanding include William James, Erich Fromm, Roberto Assagioli, Karen Horney, Carl Jung, Gordon

Allport, Harry Stack Sullivan, Carl Rogers, Rollo May, Fritz Perls, Erik Erikson, Abraham Maslow, Carol Gilligan, and Jean Baker Miller. Various terms have been used in discussing what I am calling potentializing: individuation, self-actualization, becoming, self-realization, etc. The late Abraham Maslow explored the dynamics and process of actualization in great depth. He identified a hierarchy of needs in us human beings. Our most fundamental need is for safety. In ascending order, the other "basic needs" of all persons are for belonging, love, respect, and self-esteem. Transcending these basic needs is the "meta-need" to continue growing, to actualize one's potentials. In the past, counselors and therapists have dealt mainly with people who were motivated by the pain of severe deprivation of their basic needs. The "growth motivation" in such persons was hidden by their enormous "deficiency motivation." It is in more self-actualizing people, whose basic needs are better satisfied, that the "meta-need" to continue developing their capacities is most obvious and central. They are motivated, according to Maslow, primarily by trends toward self-actualization of their potentials, and by the need to fulfill their vocation or mission.[2]

In counseling with deeply troubled people, it has become clear to me (unlike Maslow) that the growth élan often can be activated even in those suffering from prolonged deficiencies of their basic needs. In the lives of such persons, growth strivings are usually hidden from others and, more important, from themselves. The key to effective therapy with such persons is to help them discover their deep desire to begin growing again. Thus, the growth élan is a crucial factor in motivating constructive change in *all* people, not just in relatively "healthy" or well-functioning people.

Two interrelated factors bring people to counseling and to other growth experiences. The one most emphasized in the literature on therapy has been the *push* of the pain of blocked growth. The other motivating force is the *pull* of the need to grow and the subconscious hope that the satisfactions of growth will be experienced. In the past, people have waited to go for therapeutic help until the pain of their diminished growth was excruciating. Fortunately, awareness is increasing in our society that continuing growth is possible throughout one's life, and that the help of a skilled growth-facilitator (a counselor, therapist, or teacher) can accelerate this natural process. As this salutary awareness increases, more people are being attracted much sooner to growth-oriented counseling and life-enrichment experiences. They are discovering that developing their potential is inherently self-rewarding.

Growth involves both struggle and satisfaction, both pain and joy. The process of growth brings the satisfactions of developing more effective skills for living. But the process often involves struggle and pain. Growing involves risk since it means letting go of what we are (which often feels safe and comfortable) without knowing in advance what we will become.[3] Before we can experience a growth of intimacy in a close relationship, for example, we must take the risk of greater openness in that relationship. This requires lowering our defenses against getting hurt in close relationships, and that isn't easy. The same defenses that protect us from hurt also block our movement toward more transparent, authentic closeness. The willingness to risk being more vulnerable is the key that opens the door to greater intimacy.

THE DYNAMIC POWER OF HOPE

Wholeness or Growth Counseling is a hope-centered approach. Hope is a powerful but often neglected dynamic for change in us human beings. Hope allows us to risk greater vulnerability. It enables us to continue struggling when growth is blocked or is very slow. A strong, explicit emphasis on hope has been lacking in pathology-oriented therapies. When people come for help with major life crises they often feel in or near despair. The growth counselor seeks to fan their flickering spark of hope and thus help them activate the energies needed for making constructive changes. The counselor-therapist is essentially a hope-awakener. It is significant that the New Testament links hope with faith and love (see I Cor. 13:13) as crucial factors in constructive relationships. When trust and love are at a low ebb in persons and relationships, hope provides the energy by which the processes of potentializing is activated. By the power of realistic hope, trust and love can gradually grow again in the lives of despairing people.

Whether people have hope depends to a considerable extent on their expectations about their futures. The kind of future one expects has a profound influence on how one responds in the present. Hope is an indispensable resource for coping with any severe crisis. Studies of prisoners of war show that many of the deaths were the result of hopelessness. Bruno Bettelheim, in reviewing his experience in a Nazi concentration camp, observed that prisoners who became hopeless (because they believed the repeated statements of the guards that they would never leave the camp except as corpses) became like walking corpses. These prisoners stopped even trying to get food for themselves and soon died.[4] For us human beings, hope depends on a variety of factors: our expectation about the future and the meanings it holds for us, the sense of having some power to influence our environment and move toward our goals, and the attitudes of significant persons toward us and our future.

A variety of approaches are used in Growth Counseling to fan the spark of hope into a flame of energy for change. These include believing that people have the power to change; actively affirming their growth potential, their power to change; coaching them as they learn the skills of intentional change; encouraging them to picture themselves mentally as growing toward their goals; affirming even small efforts to change their situation constructively; relating to them both with caring and with confrontation. As people gradually discover that they *can* change and grow, their hope and self-esteem increase. Actualized hopes foster stronger, more realistic expectations of the future. These new feelings of hope and self-worth provide the energy for further growth.

INTENTIONALITY AND GROWTH

Unlike acorns, which will become oaks if external circumstances are favorable, we can choose to inhibit or enable our own becoming. Human growth is maximized through decision, action, and self-discipline. For example, it requires continuing choices, self-discipline, and practice for most of us to develop our potential to play a musical instrument or to become effective counselors or teachers. Creative intentionality is a key to self-growth. By the goals one chooses and the actions one takes to move toward these goals in the present, one participates in creating one's future, intentionally. To paraphrase a medieval Talmudic text: Human beings alone among the animals are incomplete, but we have the capacity to complete ourselves.[5] Intentionality is the opposite of blaming others or circumstances, the opposite of drifting and wishing that things will improve or that one will be rescued. Intentionality is using one's freedom and power, however limited or great these may be at a given point, to take responsibility for one's life. The growth counselor seeks to challenge and encourage people to live more intentionally and thereby to gradually increase their freedom and strength to choose and change.

Patricia, a participant in a growth group for young adults, put it well:

> I came to the group absolutely sure that I was the victim of my miserable childhood and all my bad breaks. This group kept pointing out that I was using that belief to keep from taking responsibility for what I do with me, now. You kept making me look at my self-sabotage. And I knew that you cared about me and wanted me to stop lousing up my life. The message took a long time to get through to me, but I think I'm starting to get back in the driver's seat of my life.

The growth counselor actively encourages people to set goals, develop workable plans for their own growth, and to make "contracts" with themselves to implement those plans. In this process, there's a fundamental respect for the ways each individual wants to change and grow. The ultimate choices about how one changes, in what directions, and at what speed are the right and responsibility of each person.

PLAYFUL INTENTIONALITY

We *can* be purposeful and active in our own growth. But focusing too strenuously and tensely on one's growth can block growth. Many of my best efforts to improve myself bog down in the futile struggle between that part of me that feels I should change and the part that fears and resists change. Only when I can relax and become open to the gentle leading of the part of me that *wants* to change does change occur.

Creative change seems to occur in the polarity between intentional choice and action, on the one hand, and relaxed, almost playful receptivity, on the other. Focusing too intensely on one's growth goals diminishes openness to oneself and to those nurturing relationships with other people, nature, and Spirit which are wellsprings of energy for change. In the Gestalt therapy workshop described earlier, it was only when I let go of my frantic struggle to improve myself and got in touch with the humorous absurdity of these efforts that I experienced liberation. When transformation came, it felt like a gift.

Unfortunately, in our culture "intentionality" often becomes captive of the work ethic. It becomes associated with heaviness and oughtness and loses its power to enable creative change. Rollo May has identified a key to avoiding this loss. In his thought, *creative* intentionality involves both willing and wishing. He declares: "Will is the capacity to organize one's self so that movement in a certain direction or toward a certain goal may take place. Wish is the imaginative playing with the possibility of some act or state occurring." Wishing supplies the imagination, the warmth, the freshness, the richness, the child's play to willing; but willing gives the self-direction and maturity which guide wishing. Without "wish," "will" loses its life-blood and vitality. May describes intentionality as "our imaginative participation in the coming day's possibilities . . . out of which comes the awareness of our capacity to form, to mold, to change ourselves and the day in relation to each other."[6]

To put this insight in the language of transactional analysis, effective intentionality results from a creative alliance between the playful, natural Child and the reality-oriented, choosing Adult. In psychosynthesis, the creative use of will involves the active imaging of what one wills. "Imaging" is seen as a means of energizing and empowering one's will.

To be creative, intentionality must be playful. Playfulness seems to activate the right hemisphere of the brain–the imaginative, intuitive side. Recently, I have found that letting myself experience the laughing inner clown is freeing and lightening. It's freeing to laugh inwardly at the absurd expectations I put on myself, to chuckle at the academic games and institutional rituals in which I participate with such seriousness, to snicker at my persistent tendency to take myself and my goals too seriously. The laughing inner clown can say "To hell with it" and chuckle at the absurd seriousness with which the institutions of which I'm a part tend to take so many things. Surprisingly, the freeing power of this inner playfulness can even help one cope with existential anxiety. The awareness of the inevitable losses and tragedies of life is transformed to some degree by inner laughter.

THE GROWTH PERSPECTIVE

A key to awakening realistic hope and activating intentionality in others is to believe in their power to change, and to affirm this power with warmth and caring. It is essential for the counselor-therapist-teacher to believe in the capacity of persons to grow *before* they're aware of that power in themselves. Seeing the well-hidden potential in growth-blocked people isn't easy. To do so requires *seeing them through the growth perspective.*

The pathology perspective, which has dominated the practice of so much counseling and therapy, tends to retard creative change. Like most counselors I invested substantial energies during my training to put on the glasses of pathology by learning to identify and diagnose "sickness" in myself and others. It isn't easy to remove these glasses. If I see those who come for therapy through this pathology perspective, I am aware mainly of their failures and hang-ups, their mistakes, lost opportunities, and areas of unfreedom. Since these factors are *there* in everyone, it's not difficult for a pathology-oriented eye to see them, especially in other people. When people are perceived primarily in terms of their pathology, they sense this at some level. Their hope is thereby diminished precisely when they need hope the most to free them to change. The counselor's negative perceptions are somehow contagious. Fortunately, hope is also contagious. If I put on the *glasses of growth*, I am able to see the pain and pathology of people in the context of their past successes (however limited), present strengths, and future potentialities. The awareness of being perceived in this affirming way seems to fan the flickering spark of realistic hope. In the first session of a mid-years renewal group Bob described himself as "a forty-seven-year-old tired businessman." His body language and his low energy level reflected his chronic, mid-years depression. But his hope for change gradually revived in the group. At the close of the eighth session he could say: "There's a lot of me I've never known was there–a lot of feelings and a lot of things I can do with the rest of my life. You [group members] believed in me a hell of a lot more than I did when we started!" Then, with obvious zest, he shared some of his new plans for his life. This group had become an *environment of hope and change* for Bob.

Psychological research has demonstrated that the expectations of significant people are powerful influences on our behavior. In the mid sixties, psychologists Robert Rosenthal and Lenore Jacobsen discovered what they called the "Pygmalion effect" in education. At the beginning of a school year they administered a nonverbal test of intelligence to all children in eighteen elementary school classes. They disguised the test by telling the teachers that it would predict which of the children would be "intellectual bloomers." They gave the teachers the names of children who "could be expected to show remarkable gains" in intellectual competence during the coming eighteen months. Actually these students were chosen at random to form the experimental group. A control group of children matching the bloomers in age, sex, and IQ scores was also selected. The only differences between the groups were in the mind of the teachers. When all the children were retested at the end of the academic year, the bloomers showed significantly greater gains in their IQ scores than the children in the control group. The positive perception and expectations of the teachers produced greater gains in bloomers at all levels of intellectual ability![7]

Since this original research, there have been more than two hundred similar studies using persons of various ages in different educational and training programs. These studies throw light on why people tend to live up to or down to the expectations of significant people in their lives. Teachers who have been led to expect exceptional growth from certain students or trainees tend to create a warmer emotional climate around those persons and put more of themselves into the relationships. There have been only a few studies of the Pygmalion effect in counseling or therapy, but, Rosenthal has stated, "I agree that therapists' expectancy can be a factor in outcome [of therapy]." It seems clear that a counselor's expectation of growth in a client, based on an awareness of that person's real potentialities, helps to energize growth in the client. Putting on the glasses of growth is the most effective way of helping all of your relationships become more growth-producing.

Wholeness counseling is much more than a set of techniques. It is, at its heart, a basic orientation toward people–a growth- and hope-centered way of perceiving, experiencing, and relating to them. The growth-hope perspective is more essential than any particular technique. Only to the extent that I am able to put on the glasses of growth will the methods I use in teaching, counseling, and growth groups be energized so that they can produce maximum growth. I find that when I have on the growth glasses, old techniques sometimes acquire fresh effectiveness. New growth methods tend to emerge spontaneously.

THE GROWTH FORMULA

Growth occurs in the tension and interplay between caring and confrontation, between love and justice, between playfulness and decision. The "growth formula" can be simply stated: GROWTH = CARING + CONFRONTATION. Growth tends to occur in any relationship–student-teacher, client-therapist, child-parent, husband-wife, parishioner-pastor, friend-friend–to the degree that two things are experienced: *caring* (acceptance, affirmation, grace, love), which one does not have to earn because it is *there* in that relationship, and *confrontation* (openness, honesty) with those aspects of reality that are being ignored or denied. Confrontation needs to focus on both negative, growth-limiting attitudes, beliefs, and behavior in persons and on the positive potential for change of which they are unaware.

Confrontation produces change only when it leads to *self*-confrontation. Without genuine caring, confrontation is experienced as rejection. This elicits defensiveness, not self-confrontation and the inner desire to change. Acceptance and love without confrontation tend to be experienced as incomplete or phoney. Growth-enabling love affirms the potentials of others and challenges them to do whatever is needed to develop those assets. A confronting challenge to grow can be as loving and as crucial to change as acceptance and affirmation. I recall a counseling relationship with Carl, a lonely, defensive man in his early thirties. After trust had grown between us, I said: "I'd like to share a hunch with you, to see if it makes any sense. I see you as a person with a lot on the ball. You're really hurting from loneliness; yet you seem to be keeping people at a distance by the up-tight way you come on. It's like you're cutting yourself off from what you want from others, keeping them at a distance. You prevent them from seeing the things they'd like in you and keep them from giving you what you need." It was my intention to affirm and confront him in the same statement. The lively interchange that followed helped him become more aware of his distancing behavior and the conflicted *need for* and *fear of* closeness, behind that behavior. He also began to sense my belief in his ability to risk changing his behavior to interrupt his self-imposed loneliness. This interaction proved to be a turning point in his therapy.

CRISES AS GROWTH OPPORTUNITIES

The wholeness counselor views crises as potential growth opportunities. Both *developmental crises*, which occur during each transition from one life stage to the next, and *accidental crises*, caused by unexpected illness, accidents, and severe losses, confront us with the painful necessity of learning new ways to meet our basic needs. The death of one's parents, for example, confronts a person at any age with the necessity of doing unfinished growth work. In my case these painful losses within the last few years have forced me to let go of some of my lingering emotional dependencies on them and to stand more firmly on my own feet. When a severe crisis strikes, life challenges us to turn to people for support, and to struggle and learn new coping skills. If we do this, we develop stronger resources for handling the next crisis which is probably just around the next turn in the road. In contrast, if we avoid facing the problem (by denial, too much busyness or booze, or other escapes), if we refuse to ask for support from others and don't learn the skills demanded by the new situation, our coping muscles are weakened. We will be less "cope-able" when the next crisis hits. Crises are times of heightened vulnerability. One stands at a fork in the path. One direction leads toward growth, the other toward diminished effectiveness in handling life constructively. People can use crises growth fully only if they can activate the energies of realistic hope in the context of caring relationships.

As a crisis counselor, I never cease to marvel at the way some people turn huge minuses into partial pluses by finding new meaning and strength in even miserable life situations. Within relationships of warmth and trust and caring, many people learn to use their personality muscles in new, strengthening ways, taking appropriate action to handle devastating problems and losses constructively. Turning a minus into a partial plus, often involves the discovery, after the worst of a crisis is over, that one's pain can be a bridge of instant rapport with others going through similar losses. Finding out that a crisis has admitted one to a warm bond of mutual caring is like an unexpected gift.

Wholeness Counseling is a developmental approach. Each life stage is both a synopsis of all that has gone before and a preface to the future. A new stage, whether we like it or not, is a growth challenge with new problems and new possibilities not available before that stage. The most effective way to handle the new problems is to develop the new possibilities of that life stage intentionally. Our youth-oriented culture makes it difficult to believe that there are fresh, exciting growth possibilities for us after forty to fifty or even, would you believe, sixty, seventy and beyond. The Pygmalion effect operates here too. Our beliefs and expectations regarding the mature years can limit or liberate the potentials we discover in ourselves and others.

PATHOLOGY, EVIL, AND GROWTH

As I reflect on what I've said about growth up to this point, I'm confronted by the other side of my experience. I think of couples in marriage therapy who seemed hopelessly locked in growth-stifling, neurotic interaction. I recall families in which interpersonal destructiveness was being transmitted like a plague from one generation to the next. I remember with sadness, persons who I have known whose lives were protracted suicides, their creative potential deeply buried under layers of accumulated deadness. I think of the rigid, castrating people I have encountered in churches who sugarcoated their destructiveness with phoney piety. Then, as if all these memories aren't enough, I think of my own resistance to doing what I know will help me grow: my backsliding from growth experiences like the one described earlier; my angry, manipulative side that hurts me and the people I care about most. Individual pathology or evil, by whatever name it's called, is a persistent reality in all our lives and relationships.

Recent history highlights the destructiveness of collective, growth-blocking evil in society. The Holocaust is a continuing confrontation, for many of us, with the depth and enormity of human evil. The grim reality of the systematic, "efficient" murder of 6 million defenseless women, men, and children in an "enlightened" society crushes any tendencies we may have toward superficial optimism about us human beings. It's relatively easy to dismiss mass atrocities in remote and less advanced cultures or periods of history. But here was a recent effort to wipe out a whole people in a country that rightly prided itself on its contributions to art and music, to science and philosophy and religion. It's impossible to explain away the Holocaust by projecting the full blame on that madman Hitler and his SS henchmen who either shared his moral insanity or were rendered powerless to disobey by their culture's exaggerated, irrational obedience to those in authority. Without the passive acquiescence of countless normal, moral people in many countries who chose to look the other way, the Nazi death-machine could not have continued its genocidal madness with relatively little resistance.

I experience the confrontation of the Holocaust on a very personal level because Germany is the land of my roots. From that country, ancestors on both sides of my family came to America. I remember the inner wrenching and revulsion I experienced after the war when I stood in the gas chambers at Auschwitz, aware that the remarkable creativity of German culture did not prevent this tragedy of collective evil. The same culture that produced Albert Schweitzer with his reverence for life, produced Hitler with his fiendish love of death.

Collective human evil is not, unfortunately, an atypical aberration in human history. The dismal story of slavery and the continuing oppression of Native Americans and women are examples of profound social evil close to home. Much as we self-righteously like to blame such social malignancies on a few bad people, the shadow of Wounded Knee and the slave block and witch burning, of Mai Lai, Watergate, and the former Yugoslavia, are in us all. The current epidemic of violence reflected in widespread child abuse, battering of women, and rape is but one contemporary expression of human destructiveness. Comparable examples could be cited from other cultures and periods of history.

Why do so few of us use more than a fraction of our potentialities? Why are most of us so ingenious at hurting one another and sabotaging ourselves? Why do we suffer from severely truncated growth, from crippling in our close relationships? Why do we contribute to the continuing exploitation of powerless people and nations? Why do we settle for self-damaging life-styles and values? Why do we all have some wounded, messy, destructive sides to our lives? These questions defy easy answers, but they must be faced.

To be effective, growth-oriented approaches to people must be utterly honest in facing the prevalence of evil and pathology in individuals and families, in institutions and society. We will be effective in helping people liberate their potentials only if we take the depth of human destructiveness, pathology, and resistance to growth seriously. The "human potential" obviously includes an enormous potential for destructiveness as well as creativity. Growth can be cancerous. Change can be malignant, a vicious circle of self-destructiveness.

Clearly we human beings are strange mixtures of the transcendent and the tragic, of freedom and trappedness, of wholeness and brokenness, of creativity and chaos. No facile optimism or general pessimism can provide an adequate understanding of the contradictions and complexities, the misery and the grandeur of our humanity.

Human destructiveness has been seen by some thinkers as inherent and therefore inevitable. It has been attributed to "original sin" (as in traditional Christian theology) or "the death instinct" (by Freud). Some such views of human evil and pathology simply reinforce a sense of hopelessness, helplessness, and resignation, a passive waiting to be rescued by God or by science.[8] Such "waiting for Godot" responses tend to lessen active, responsible, growthful coping with the reality and power of human destructiveness.

It is much more illuminating and constructive, as a working hypothesis, to understand personal and family pathology as resulting from grossly diminished or deeply blocked growth. Instead of "psychological illness," I prefer, with Maslow, the concept of "human diminution or stunting."[9] When human potentializing is blocked in a deep, protracted way, that life energy is subverted and expressed in distorted, malignant ways. It is because we humans have such remarkable potential for creativity that we are capable of such monstrous atrocities against ourselves and one another. Our vast destructiveness can be understood at least in part as a caricature of our enormous potential for creativity. When the growth élan is deeply blocked, we develop a wide variety of symptoms: neuroses, psychoses, character disorders, addictions, psychosomatic disorders, mutually damaging relationships, and such social pathologies as racism, sexism, and chauvinistic nationalism. Much of the destructiveness in the lives of individuals is a malignant self-protest of the waste of their potentials. Furthermore, much of our collective, societal destructiveness can be understood in an evolutionary perspective as an expression of the unfinishedness of individuals and cultures. Deeply diminished potentializing and the incompleteness of the evolutionary process may not prove to be fully adequate explanations of all human destructiveness, especially collective destructiveness. But, it will be utterly impossible to determine what part of our destructiveness is from these sources until we develop a society in which our institutions, groups, and relationships generally support rather than stymie human becoming.

In the meantime, it is important to put pathology and other forms of destructiveness in the broader context of hope for change. To see the negative side of our lives in the context of hope for positive transformation is the most effective way to energize the process of constructive change. It is truly remarkable how some people respond when one approaches their destructive pathology with growth-centered understanding and methods of change. As the rage and despair, the guilt and the grief of unlived life are diminished and as people learn how to live more growthfully, their destructiveness often diminishes drastically. As they begin to use more of their potential, the destructive energy seems to be transformed as if it were rechanneled into growing. Such transformations usually will not occur unless someone who accepts and cares about them enough to comfort them, believes that changes are indeed possible.

It's remarkable what one sees, even in severe pathology, when one risks seeing people through bifocal glasses–the bottom lens seeing brokenness and pathology, the top lens seeing hope and growth possibilities. For nearly three decades I have worked with alcoholics and their families. It boggles my mind to realize how slowly the light of the growth perspective dawned for me in that area. One evening, only a few years ago, as I prepared for a workshop the next day, I reviewed in my memory the recovering alcoholics whom I had known over the years. I was troubled by the dim awareness that something crucial was missing in my understanding of the recovery process. I went to bed and slept fretfully until about 4:00 a.m. I awoke suddenly with an "Aha!" feeling. I became aware of what should have been obvious to me years before–that I had never known an alcoholic who recovered who had not begun to grow again psychologically, interpersonally, and spiritually. As I reflected on this, it gradually became clear that behind the chronic, excessive drinking that led to the entrapment of addiction, there was a profound sense of unlived life. Thus, for me, the growth perspective threw new light on both the prevention and the recovery processes in addictions.

As I think of the variety of human pain I have encountered in counseling relationships and growth groups over the years–depression; low self-esteem; anxiety states; food, drug, and work addiction; chronic depleted energy; sexual diminution and hang-ups; marriage and family problems; psychosomatic problems; value emptiness and confusion; fear of death; meaninglessness; pathological religion, to mention only a few–I have a startling awareness. Behind these varied "presenting problems" there was a common complaint: a profound sense of unlived life. Symptoms develop when we feel that we're not growing, not creating, not living authentically! Theodore Roszak puts it well when he describes psychopathology as the "wounding discrepancies between potentiality and actuality."[10]

Many of us learn to express our growth strivings in grotesque, distorted ways. For example, people who have learned to equate feeling worthwhile and strong (which are legitimate human needs) with possessing things, scramble endlessly to acquire money and possessions. Often they continue to do so even if their physical, mental, and spiritual health and their close relationships are terribly damaged by the process. In scrambling compulsively for things, they cut themselves off from the genuine relational sources of self-esteem and joy in living.

When the malignant pathology of severely diminished and distorted growth has continued for years, it requires an enormous investment of therapeutic skill and energy to liberate the person to grow again. In many cases, our present level of therapeutic expertise is inadequate for the task. But one should never decide in advance that growth is hopelessly blocked in certain individuals. Such a hopeless mind-set may blind us to the growth of which those persons would be capable if they were seen through the growth perspective.

As suggested above, the glasses of growth must be *bifocals*. The lower lens must see clearly the painful pathology of blocked growth that brings people to counseling. But the upper and larger lens must focus on the wider context–the strengths and potentials they also possess. It is as unrealistic and ineffective to see only potentials as it is to see only pathology. But to be aware of the background strengths and potentials of people, as one attends to their pain and pathology in the foreground, energizes hope and growth. The energy of realistic hope is activated in both sides of a helping relationship by this way of perceiving.

THE COMPLEMENTARITY OF COUNSELING AND EDUCATION

Education and counseling are natural allies. Both have a common aim: to maximize whole-person growth. The goal of all creative education is potentializing. The word *educate* comes from the Latin, meaning to draw out one's potential. Counseling and therapy aim at *re*-education to help growth-diminished people to learn more constructive values, attitudes, and relationship skills. Growth-oriented therapy seeks to repair the capacity to learn and grow in everyday relationships and learning situations.

The complementarity of marriage enrichment and marriage counseling illustrates the possibilities of such an alliance. Marriage enrichment is essentially personalized education in relationship-building skills "to make good marriages better." Couples who participate regularly in marriage enrichment are engaging in positive prevention of marital problems. Marriage-enrichment classes, workshops, and retreats provide a group environment within which couples are helped to use the normal stresses and crises of their relationship as growth opportunities rather than letting unfaced problems accumulate and their distancing increase. My experience suggests that couples who really need marriage therapy but who participate in marriage-enrichment events, often recognize their need and seek professional help sooner than would otherwise be the case. Furthermore, an ongoing support-nurture group (one form of enrichment) for couples who have "graduated" from effective marriage counseling or therapy can help them continue the growth begun in the counseling relationship. The long-range benefits of marital therapy can be doubled by encouraging follow-on marriage enrichment.

Many "normal" people who do not need counseling or therapy to cope with severe crises or deep psychological crippling are living at only a fraction of their potentials. The strategy of Growth Counseling is to combine therapeutic and educative approaches in order to attract such people into life-enrichment and effectiveness-in-living groups.

I am not depreciating the importance of effective psychotherapy. As a recipient of as well as a practitioner of therapy, I know how vital it can be when one's growth is diminished by multiple crises and/or by early-life experiences. But if we counselors and therapists concentrate most of our energies on repair work, we are fighting a losing battle. We also need to develop more imaginative and widely available approaches to prevention. To adapt a familiar figure of speech, we must provide a fence of higher-level wellness across the top of the cliff as well as a growth repair-station at the bottom for those who suffer the brokenness of severely diminished growth. To do this we must rethink our professional priorities so that we will invest at least as much energy in preventive-wholeness work as in counseling and therapy.

MUTUAL GROWTH NETWORKS

There's an enormous, barely tapped growth resource in the countless people in your community who have handled crises and losses constructively. Every person who has grown as a result of coping effectively with demanding life experiences–e.g., getting married, having a baby, coping with the mid years, retiring, losing a mate in death or divorce, having cancer, moving to a new community, rearing a disabled child, losing an important job, recovering from an addiction, etc.–is a potential care-giver and growth-enabler for others going through similar crises. The thing that's needed in our urbanized societies is not a huge increase of therapists and professional growth-facilitators. What's needed in our rootless, mobile, faceless cities is a network of mutual-nurture groups led by trained lay persons who are warm and caring and who have grown by coping constructively with their own crises. Networks of such groups in congregations and schools, are desperately needed to replace the support no longer offered most urban dwellers by extended families, neighborhoods, and villages.

The potential of mutual-growth groups already is being actualized in exciting ways in the proliferating lay self-other help groups, many of which are modeled on Alcoholics Anonymous, the grandparent of such approaches. But the growth of millions of other people who experience severe accidental and developmental crises could be nurtured more effectively if many more self-other help groups of all kinds were available. What one could call the "AA principle" is the truth that helping others grow contributes to one's own continuing growth. This principle needs to be implemented in an expanding network of caring groups in every community. Professional counselors and therapists can have key roles in liberating the growth-nurturing power of ordinary people. Our task is to provide training, coaching, and ongoing support for lay growth-enablers. They can lead the network of mutual-growth groups in communities and in people-serving institutions. By training and coaching lay growth-enablers, we can multiply the growth impact of our professional work by geometric progression.

HUMAN WHOLENESS CENTERS

It's not enough for us as individual counselors-therapists-teachers to function in growth-center ways, as important as that is. Beyond this, our society desperately needs more institutions that function as human wholeness centers. Four networks of people-serving institutions, which already exist in most communities, have strategic roles in enabling our society to become more growth nurturing–churches and synagogues, schools on all age levels, counseling agencies, and health-care institutions. A strategy of positive prevention in your community involves making a wide variety of growth opportunities easily available through these institutions, at the lowest possible cost (or on a prepaid basis), within walking distance from where people live and work. Institutions of these four types can become more effective wholeness-centers by offering a variety of growth-oriented classes, workshops, playshops, training events, crisis support groups, growth seminars and retreats, and self-other help groups. The leadership of such growth groups and events can be provided mainly by trained lay and paraprofessional facilitators supported by growth-oriented teachers, counselors, and therapists.

I have described elsewhere a strategy for developing growth groups as a means of transforming our people-centered institutions into growth centers.[11] A brief overview will suffice here. These institutions have a wealth of facilities, personnel, and resources in most communities. Many of their leaders are trained, to some degree, in interpersonal growth skills. Many others are open to learning new ways of helping their institutions become centers of lifelong, whole-person growth. In many places in this country and elsewhere in the world, churches, schools, counseling and health agencies are becoming aware of the enormous growth yearnings of people. When the leaders and the professional staff of such institutions catch a fresh guiding vision that puts "people making" (Virginia Satir's term) at the center of their programs, exciting things begin to happen. These institutions become environments for nurturing hope and growth.

The growth approach is a "natural" for churches and synagogues. Here are eight important assets, possessed by such religious institutions, which make the growth approach an ideal model for effective ministry.

(1) Churches and synagogues have a heritage of insights about healing, growth, values, beliefs and life-styles, which can be valuable resources in developing growth groups. (2) More than any other institutions in our society, churches and synagogues have regular, face-to-face relationships with millions of "normal" people throughout the life cycle. This asset, which we usually take for granted, creates superb opportunities to develop growth-nurturing groups for people of all ages within a congregation. (3) Clergy have innumerable and strategic contacts with persons in those normal life crises which can become opportunities for personal growth. (4) Most churches and synagogues already have small groups which give support and caring to people of all ages. The effectiveness of such groups can be increased dramatically by training their leaders in growth-enabling leadership skills. (5) The presence of many natural growth facilitators among the lay members of congregations is another potential asset. Such persons can be recruited, trained and coached by the minister and by mental health professionals in the congregation, as members of care-giving teams and facilitators of mutual-growth groups. (6) Most religious leaders recognize that *spiritual* growth is central to all human growth and that enabling spiritual growth is the unique mission of religious organizations. (7) Thousands of clergy have had some training in counseling and small group methods. Many others are eager to get the supervised training that will enable them to increase their skill as whole-person *spiritual growth enablers*. (8) A growing number of clergy have had graduate training in counseling and psychotherapy which equips them as specialists in pastoral counseling. These specialists within the ministry, with their dual training in theological and psychotherapeutic disciplines, have a key role in helping congregations become more effective human-wholeness centers. To the extent that these specialists

are growth-oriented, they hold the key to providing training in growth methods for both seminary students and clergy. It is high time that the expertise of these specialists in value and spiritual growth issues also be made available to persons in other counseling and psychotherapeutic professions who lack training in these areas.[12]

To be relevant to the mainstream of human needs in the last quarter of this century, churches and synagogues must become effective spiritual wholeness centers, nurturing growth throughout the life cycle. Congregations that are moving in growth-oriented directions are, in my experience, places of high energy. Unfortunately, in many congregations, dogmatism and moralism, authoritarian and patriarchial leadership, prevent their becoming effective growth centers. Only as there are liberating changes in the leadership of such institutions will it be possible for them to move toward becoming wholeness centers.

In a more growth-enabling society, learning opportunities would be easily and inexpensively available for everyone who wanted them, throughout the stages of life. Obviously schools must play an increasing role in making such opportunities for lifelong learning more readily available. Growth-producing education involves learning how to learn, wrestling with and solving real problems, developing one's own unique creativity, expanding the horizons of one's understanding, and mastering the relationship skills that one must have to live fulfillingly with others. Growth-enabling education is learning by doing. Real learning is much more apt to occur if the teacher discovers what individual students really need and what they therefore *want* to learn. Creative education is both life centered and learner-oriented.

The yearning to learn is a central dimension of the growth élan in people. How sad that this yearning is often squelched by what happens in educational institutions. Creative learning enables people to increase both their self-esteem and their sense of competence. As a teacher it is essential that I believe in the capacity of my students to learn and grow in their own unique ways and that I communicate this belief to them. A hope-enabling teacher needs to believe in the growth capacity of students more than they can yet believe in this capacity in themselves.

There are pressing needs in our society for making more readily available the healing work to which counseling and health agencies devote their major energies. Such vital work is more effective if the agencies that provide these services function as *health* centers rather than exclusively as *sickness* centers. Fortunately, the contemporary surge of interest in whole-person health and family medicine is helping to broaden the thinking of many health professionals. When the growth-wholeness perspective of whole-person health and family medicine becomes central in counseling and health agencies, the effectiveness of their therapeutic efforts tends to increase. Basic real-locations of staff time in such settings is essential in order to provide leadership for preventive growth groups and for support groups to follow treatment. Growth-oriented mental health agencies can increase the impact for wholeness of the schools and churches in their community by helping train teachers and clergy in growth-group-facilitator skills.

Jean Baker Miller has identified a key to increasing the commitment of our institutions to human development.[13] In our culture, as in most cultures, the nurturing of others' growth has been consigned mainly to women. Therefore, it is treated by men as an activity of secondary importance–a part of "women's work." The decision-making power and leadership of our major public institutions have been mainly in the hands of men, for most of whom nurturing growth has not been a primary value or concern. It is unlikely that many of our churches, schools, counseling and health agencies will make growth their central concern until those who have the most depth experience in and concern for human development–i.e., women–share fully in redefining institutional priorities and programs. It is also of great importance that the men, who now have much of the power in our public institutions, come to share and value that power and learn from the experiences of women as our culture's primary nurturers.

LIBERATING THE LIBERATORS

As I think back over my own training and personal therapy, I'm struck by the fact that the teachers, supervisors, and therapists who most stimulated my personal and professional growth were themselves struggling, hopeful, growing persons. Personal growth is contagious. It's *caught* as much as it's *taught*. This fact has sobering implications. It's crucial that we attend to our own continuing growth work and that we not allow overinvestment in "helping others" to become an escape from self-care. If, as counselors, therapists, and teachers, we are to be liberators of human potentialities, we must take responsibility for liberating the liberators!

There's a comfortable illusion that counseling and therapy consist of one group of people, the "healthy" ones, reaching down to help others, the "sick" ones. Actually, this hierarchical conception of the counselor-client relationship is counterproductive to growth in both parties. In contrast to the old medical model of an expert helping a relatively passive recipient of services, the growth model is essentially participatory and egalitarian. It sees counseling as teaching people to mobilize their own coping resources to help themselves. Growth counselors should, in each relationship, aim at working themselves out of a job, as quickly as possible. Our authority as growth facilitators cannot be the authority of titles, degrees, or professional status, since such authority is counterproductive to growth in others and in ourselves. Our authority must be what Erich Fromm called "the authority of competence"–the authority of a skillful, caring, vulnerable, learning, and growing person.

My most liberating discovery in doing growth-centered counseling and teaching is how much it's possible to learn from clients and students. Furthermore, nothing is more growth-enabling for them! To know that your therapist or teacher respects your insights and is open to learn from you, liberates the relationship from the one-up/one-down games that diminish growth in so much education and therapy. As Carl Jung once observed, an indication of an effective therapeutic relationship is that both parties change and grow.

As a counselor, the first and most important person for you to see through the bifocal growth-hope perspective is *yourself!* Only as you become aware of your problems and rich potentials will you be able to see clearly the problems and potentials in others. The Pygmalion effect functions powerfully with respect to our expectations about ourselves. The perceptions and expectations of others can influence us only to the extent that they change our self-perceptions and self-expectations. Seeing ourselves through the growth-hope perspective activates the energies of creative change in us and in our relationships with others.

All of us are "wounded healers."[14] To be a growing person is to be in touch with one's pain and to be aware of one's hang-ups. As finite human beings, our becoming is always in process, always incomplete. The unfinishedness of our own growth will interfere with our facilitating growth in others only if we are unaware of it or pretend to ourselves and others that we "have it made." Our pain and unfinished growth will be either a *bridge* or a *barrier* to the pain and unfinished growth of others. If we ignore these or pretend that they are not there, they will be barriers in relating to growth-needing people. But if we risk being vulnerable about our own pain and growth struggles, these can become a bridge of understanding, an empathetic link to the pain and growth needs of others. Your most precious asset is your authentic imperfect self. For people whose growth has been diminished by inauthentic relating, your *being there* with caring, as yourself, with your imperfections, is what they most need to awaken the growth strivings in them.

EXPERIENCING GROWTH AS LIBERATION

The goal of growth counseling has been described as the liberation of the potentialities of persons in all dimensions of their lives, beginning with inner liberation. Let me invite you to experience some aspects of inner liberation by a guided imagery exercise that can be used in counseling and other growth experiences.[15] I have found this exercise helpful in my own growth struggles.

Have someone read the instructions, stopping at each slash (/) long enough for you to do unhurriedly what has been suggested. After you have finished the experience, reverse roles and give the other person an opportunity to do the exercise.

> Get comfortable; close your eyes. / Be aware of your feelings about doing this exercise. / Stretch and relax. / Be aware of your breathing and of the sensations in your body. / Now, in your imagination, picture yourself inside a closed box. Be in

the box. / Push on the sides of your box; experience being boxed in. How does your body feel now? / Examine your box, looking for a way out. / If you've found a way, get out of the box now. / If you're still in the box, invite someone to help you get out, being aware of how it feels to ask for help. / Be alone in a beautiful, warm, spring meadow. Let yourself enjoy the freedom, the sun, the openness of the meadow. Enjoy yourself in whatever ways you choose. / Be aware of differences between your feelings now and when you were in the box. How does your body feel? / Invite your best friend to enjoy the meadow with you for a while, being aware of how this changes your experience. / Send that person away and be alone again in the meadow. How do you feel now? / In the distance, see a volcano that is about to erupt. Move as close as you wish to watch the eruption. / Be aware of changes in your feelings. / Let the eruption gradually subside until the volcano is quiet. / Return to the beautiful meadow and enjoy it again. / Recall how you looked as a child. Bring that child into the meadow to enjoy it with yourself as an adult. Play together in the free space of the meadow. / Do something to show your liking of yourself as a child. / Hold the child tenderly. Communicate your love and esteem. / Now go back to the place where you left the box. How do you feel about it now? / Do whatever you want with your box. / Before you open your eyes, reflect on your experience. In your actual life, what reminds you of your experience in the box? in the meadow? / How does your lifestyle cause you to feel boxed in? free? What things in society, in our institutions, box you in? help you feel free? / What have you learned about your pent-up negative feelings? your inner trappedness and freedom? the things you need to liberate yourself from? / Is a part of your creativity trapped in that box? in the volcano? / How do you feel about your experiences with your inner child? What do you choose to do about what you've learned in this exercise? / When you are ready, gently open your eyes. / Discuss your experience with the other person. / If you found this meaningful, I suggest that you try it several times during the next few weeks, being aware of changes in your experiences.

Chapter 3

The Flow and Methods
of Wholeness Counseling

To illustrate how the principles described in the preceding two chapters can be applied in the practice of counseling, let's look at a counseling relationship in which growth-oriented methods are used. This is a composite case created from several counseling relationships in which I have been involved. Such a composite case is a teaching device that protects confidentiality and yet retains some of the realism of an actual counseling relationship. My hope is that this chapter will illuminate the process by which the counselor-therapist facilitates creative change in the lives of two persons and in their relationships. Because the primary focus is on what counselors can do to facilitate growth, I am aware of citing many more counselor responses than client responses. This may give the erroneous impression that the counselor directs the interaction more than actually happens in effective counseling or therapy. Growth work is done, it should be emphasized, by the *clients* with the encouragement and coaching of the counselor. My comments about the counselor's intentions and the dynamics of the counseling appear in brackets. Near the close of the chapter, I'll summarize what I regard as the crucial methods used to facilitate the growth process.

I have selected counseling material from work with couples who were committed to their relationships and relatively open to change so that growth will be more rapid and the dynamics of growth easier to recognize. The danger of creating a composite case from work with such open, strongly motivated people is that it may sound too good to be true. I need to emphasize that the majority of people whom I have seen for counseling were more resistant to change than this couple. Growth-oriented methods are no less useful with them, but change usually is more labored, gradual, and partial than in this case. I must also make it clear that many of the methods described in this chapter are the established methods of relational marriage counseling. They are used here with a robust and explicit growth orientation and emphasis.

The counseling relationship began on the telephone when Sue, age 27, called a church-sponsored counseling and growth center and talked to Pete, a minister with advanced training in psychotherapy and marriage counseling. After hearing that Sue was seeking counseling, Pete asked, "Would you tell me a little about the problem, please?" [This request sought to discover whether there was an acute crisis demanding immediate help. It also served to get information on the basis of which Pete could decide who to invite to the first counseling session.]

> **Sue** (with heaviness in her voice): I don't know where to begin. Things have been going downhill between my husband and me. I guess I'm really the problem. Sometimes I feel like I'm going to climb the walls, I feel so depressed!
> **Pete:** It sounds as if things are really heavy. I'm glad you decided to call to get some help with the load you're carrying. It takes strength to be willing to ask for help when you need it. [Pete's intention was to begin to awaken Sue's hope by letting her know that he heard her pain and affirmed the constructive action she had already taken by seeking professional help.]
> **Sue** (after she poured out more of her painful feelings): Can I make an appointment to see you about this–soon?
> **Pete:** Yes, I'll be glad to see you. But since some of your pain relates to your marriage, I think it would be helpful if I could see both of you, for at least a session or two. How would you feel about having a few joint sessions, if your husband is willing?

Sue responded that that was acceptable and that her husband, Jerry, probably would be willing to come, provided it didn't take a lot of his time.

> **Sue:** He's in a graduate program in business administration at the university, working night and day on a special project. I

don't want to interfere with that.

Pete: Sounds like you're both under a lot of pressure.

Sue: But I *should* be able to cope with my end of things better. I give Jerry a lot of flack that he doesn't deserve or need–

Pete:–which makes you feel more down on yourself.

Sue: Yes, for sure.

After a few minutes of conversation, Pete made a tentative appointment to see the couple the next evening. It was agreed that Sue would come alone if Jerry refused or was busy. Sue called later and confirmed a joint appointment.

In the first counseling session, after a brief description of their problems in getting a baby-sitter, Pete asked Jerry: "How did you feel when Sue told you I would like to see you both at least for a session or two?" [Because Jerry had not asked for help for himself, it was essential to build rapport with him by listening to his feelings, particularly any pain or negative feelings.]

> **Jerry:** Surprised, I guess, and a little ticked off. The thought that went through my head was, "With *my* schedule can't she even handle her counseling by herself?" But I'm willing to do it if it'll help her feel better.
>
> **Pete:** I appreciate your openness about how you felt about coming. I can understand how it would seem like one more demand on your time. But I sense that you're really concerned about the problems Sue's having. I'm glad you were willing to come, in spite of your resistance. [The counselor wanted to let Jerry know that he heard and respected his resistance but that he also affirmed the caring that seemed to be behind his choosing to come.]
>
> **Jerry:** Yes, we had a good thing going until the last few months. Then all hell broke loose. She's had a lot of trouble getting herself together.
>
> **Pete:** It must be difficult for both of you. I sense that you'd like to get back the good things you've lost. [Pete's intention was to recognize their faint hope and thus to reinforce it.]
>
> **Jerry:** I would! (Sue nodded in agreement.) I thought things were going to be OK after Dickie came, but they've been a mess! (Jerry continued to pour out his anger.)

Pete: You've been carrying quite a load of disappointment and anger, Jerry. How do you feel about what Jerry's been saying, Sue? [Pete probably moved away from Jerry's anger too rapidly at this point.]

Sue: Sorry that he has to be involved in this. I should be making things easier for him when he's under so much pressure in his work. (She continued to ventilate her guilt and feelings of failure as a wife and mother.) [It was essential for the counselor to hear and to respond with warmth and empathy to the pain that Jerry and Sue were feeling. As they poured out their feelings and their perceptions of the crisis, it became clear to Pete that Jerry was more open about his own hurt than was evident at the outset when both Sue and Jerry were describing the problem as *her* depression.]

Pete: Let me say why I wanted to see both of you. It has been my experience that when one person is hurting a lot in a close relationship, both people are usually feeling pain and contributing to each other's pain in some way. Working together in counseling often is the best way for them to deal with the problems that are causing the pain. [Sensing that Jerry might be open to joint counseling, Pete sought in this mildly confronting statement to explain why it might be helpful for them both to be involved.]

Jerry: I guess I haven't been the easiest person to live with lately. [Jerry's relaxation of his defense of projecting the problem onto Sue was seen by Pete as very hopeful.]

Pete: You've been feeling a lot of pressure.

Jerry: Yeah, I've been as up-tight as hell about a lot of things.

Pete: I get the impression life is a pressure cooker for *both* of you right now. Your graduate program sounds heavy, Jerry, plus your worries about Sue. And it's a rough time for you, Sue, with the heavy demands of a baby, especially when you're feeling down on yourself. It must feel to both of you like the roof has fallen in on you.

Jerry: Yeah, it's been heavy for both of us since Dickie came. Actually things started deteriorating right after she resigned her job, a couple of months before he was born.

Sue: I had taught math at the local high school for five years before that.

Pete: You miss your teaching?

Sue: I miss the discipline hassles like a hole in the head. But, yes, I got a lot out of teaching besides the money, which we certainly could use now. Some of the kids and the other teachers were neat people.

Pete: You've had a double loss–not being able to bring in money you need and losing all the satisfactions you got from teaching. No wonder you're feeling down. [The counselor's intention was to help Sue identify her depressed feelings as including grief and to recognize the appropriateness of her feelings of loss.]

Later in the session Sue commented: "I guess I really haven't faced how much I miss all the good things about my career."

Pete: It's obvious that you've both had a variety of difficult adjustments and losses recently. Some important satisfactions have evaporated, and a lot of new pressures have hit you. Apparently you both feel you've lost many of the good things you had going in your marriage before Dickie came along.

Jerry: Yes, we had our ups and downs, like everybody does. But the four years before Dickie came were good ones. (Sue nods in agreement.)

Pete: It's hopeful that you had those good years. You can't go back to that same space, since circumstances have changed, but you both know from experience that you *can* do much better. You may be able to build on that knowledge to make things better for both of you. [Pete was seeking to help them see the realistic hope in their having demonstrated the capacity for a more mutually satisfying relationship. That a couple agree in their general perception of how their crisis developed is also a positive sign. This usually indicates that their reality-perceiving ability is not severely distorted by their pain.]

Sue: Things would be a lot better if we'd been ready for this. (In the discussion that followed this comment, it developed that they had not planned to start their family until Jerry finished his graduate program two years hence. Jerry expressed his anger at Sue for "not being more careful," and Sue, her guilt about forgetting to take her pill on several occasions.) [By responding to their feelings, Pete encouraged them both to express their festering feelings about the unplanned pregnancy.]

Pete: You've been storing up a lot of anger about the pregnancy, Jerry. And you seem to be giving yourself a very bad time about this, Sue. The fact that the baby was unplanned threw both of you a curve, didn't it?

Jerry: It sure did! [This catharsis continued; when it seemed to have run its course, Pete summarized some of his impressions.]

Pete: Let me give you some feedback of what I think I'm picking up, to check it out with you. You're both feeling very angry and deprived in your relationship, you're expressing your pain in ways that make it almost impossible for the other person to meet your needs. It's as if you've got a blame-guilt cycle going between you. You're feeling heavy grief and a sense of failure, Sue. Your anger about the pregnancy, Jerry, makes it easy for you to clobber her, which makes you feel guiltier and more put down, Sue. All this makes it harder for you to cope with Dickie or to respond to Jerry's needs. When you withdraw into your depression, Sue, it's even harder for Jerry to give you the emotional support you need. Does either of you get the feeling that you're pushing the other person away just when you need all the love and support you can get? [Pete's intention in this overly long summary was to increase their awareness of the futility of the self-sabotaging cycle in which they were caught, thus confronting them with the need to find more mutually satisfying ways of relating. Such a confrontation can be premature if it interrupts the pouring out of the client's anger.]

Jerry: We surely are getting further apart all the time, like we're living in two separate worlds—with a damn wall between us. [It's hopeful that the pain behind Jerry's anger continued to emerge after Pete's wordy intervention.]

Pete: You're feeling a lot of loneliness, Jerry. That really feels heavy.

Jerry: (turning to look at Sue for the first time in the session): I guess it's pretty stupid to keep clobbering you about the pregnancy–makes it tougher for you to pull out of your low. (Tears came to Sue's eyes.)

Pete (after some moments of silence): Jerry, I'm really touched by what you just did. That took guts. (Sue reached out and touched Jerry's hand.) The pain you're both feeling in this crisis is a signal that you need to make some constructive changes. From the way you've responded to each other in this session, I have a hunch that you've got a lot going for you in your marriage, at least potentially, a lot you can use to interrupt the self-defeating cycle you're in and have your needs for closeness met better. [Pete's purpose was to challenge them with the needed change at the same time that he strengthened their hope by affirming their capacity to change.] How do you feel about this?

Sue (smiling): Much more hopeful–like we *can* improve things. And the load doesn't feel like it's all on me to change.

Jerry: I feel better too.

Pete invited each of them to describe more concretely what needed to change in their relationship to make things better for them. This allowed them to begin to relate the reduction of their pain to specific changes in their behavior. Toward the end of the session, Pete said: "It's obvious that you've been hurting each other a lot over the last few months. Would you be willing to try looking at the other side of your feelings for a few minutes, to see what's there?" (They agreed.) "OK, in spite of your pain, what is good in your marriage, what is there that you still like and appreciate about the other person? Take turns telling the other what these things are. Who wants to start?" Jerry listened as Sue listed a number of things she appreciated in him and in their marriage. After she finished, Jerry told her the things he appreciated in her. Pete watched as their eyes lighted up during their mutual affirmation. Both appeared surprised and pleased by what they heard. When they finished, Pete shared his feelings: "I was really touched as I listened to you. I feel a warm glow inside me. In spite of your crisis, you obviously still have a lot going *for* you, a lot to build on."

This exercise can help some couples begin to extricate themselves from mutual hurting and distancing. For couples who still do care about each other (however ambivalently), this structured mutual affirmation can help interrupt the cycles by providing a "feast" to feed their deep emotional hungers. However, the exercise can be effective only if the timing is right. It should be used only after the anger and hurt have been reduced by being expressed and worked through to some extent. Until that happens most couples aren't even aware of the things they still like in each other. If couples do not respond to this exercise, it is usually because it has been suggested too soon or because they are very deeply alienated.

Before the session ended, Sue and Jerry discussed and decided to follow Pete's suggestion that they have five more joint sessions to work on their relationship and that they also each have a few individual sessions to explore their personal issues and needs.

> **Pete:** If you can both feel that you're doing some growing and improving of your self-support, it may be easier to improve things in your relationship. I suspect that a lot of your turmoil and depression, Sue, is related to your grief that your options have been drastically reduced recently, because your career was interrupted.

It was understood that, at the end of their series of sessions, they would evaluate what had happened and decide whether to continue counseling. [This process of "contracting" is an essential aspect of firming up a counseling relationship. The purpose of asking them to commit themselves to an initial series of sessions was to give them a block of time to heal their alienation and strengthen their mutual need satisfaction.]

At the end of the session, Pete asked, "How do you feel about what we've done in this session?" They agreed that although it wasn't what they had expected, they each felt more hopeful and less burdened. [It is important for a counselor to get such evaluative feedback from clients frequently, particularly in early sessions. Asking for feedback communicates respect for the counselees' feelings and helps them bring out unfinished issues and negative feelings.]

Pete: I'm aware of warm feelings, as I think about working together. I really like your openness and what I sense is your commitment to working this through to make things better for both of you and for Dickie. I'm looking forward to getting to know you better.

Jerry: I need to say there's another side to my feelings about Dickie. He's quite a kid, and I'm glad we have him–most of the time. (smiling)

Sue: Sometimes when I'm nursing him and he looks up at me the way he does, I melt inside.

Pete: You both have some positive feelings toward Dickie, even though his joining your family when he did has been rough. It's good for him, that you like having him–most of the time–and that you're honest with yourself about your other feelings. [Apparently the earlier exploration of their resentment and guilt about the pregnancy pushed them to express the other side of their conflicted feelings.] By the way, I was aware that some of the feelings you were expressing earlier, Jerry, were familiar to me. They reminded me of some things that went on in me when our first child was born. It may be more difficult for me as a man, I suspect, to understand some of your feelings, Sue. If I'm going to help both of you, I can't be on one person's side. So I hope you'll say so if you feel I'm not understanding you, Sue. [Pete was seeking to guard against the danger inherent in one's easier identification with the client of the same sex by recognizing the danger openly and asking for Sue's help in avoiding it.]

As between-session homework, Pete recommended that they do two things: to get two notebooks to serve as "growth logs" in which they would record significant insights and learning experiences; and to repeat the exercise of telling each other what they appreciated. [Such homework is designed to encourage people to continue their growth work between sessions, thereby discovering that they *can* do it without the counselor's help. In this situation, after a first session, it would have been better if Pete had suggested only one task.]

The couple came ten minutes late for the second session. They looked discouraged. They had been "too busy" to do the home-work. As they described their cold distancing during the week, Pete became aware of Jerry's continuing resistance and resentment.

> **Pete:** It seems that I missed the boat last time, Jerry, by not being aware of where you were coming from with your feel-ings. I was asking you to move very fast from seeing the problem as Sue's to seeing it as also yours and to being willing to get involved in doing something to change things. Even though you might accept with your head what I said about the vicious cycle you both are contributing to, it isn't easy to shift gears, particularly when much more than you expected is being asked of you. You must have felt really pushed by me to let go of the feeling that everything would be OK if only Sue would get her act together. [Pete's intention in this response was to "own" his lack of sensitivity to Jerry's hidden anger at the drastic shift he had been asked to make in redefining who needed counseling.]
> **Jerry:** Yeah, I didn't even level with myself about my feelings at the end of the last session. I was a little pissed off, I guess.
> **Pete:** I have a hunch you were feeling more than a little.
> **Jerry:** Not really. It wasn't that big a deal. (Pete sensed Jerry's continuing denial of his anger toward him. He accepted his need for this denial but stayed with his feelings and gradually helped him express his real ambivalence about being in coun-seling. The interaction that followed gave Jerry a chance to work through some of his resistance. This process continued, to a diminishing degrees, for several sessions.)

As they talked about their struggles during the week, their loneli-ness and desire to have more time together came up several times. They agreed that this was a shared need they both wanted to work on. With Pete's coaching, they negotiated a "change plan" de-signed to help meet this need. They agreed to spend a half hour at least twice during the coming week, after Dickie had gone to bed, to "reconnect" by sharing significant experiences from the day. They also decided to plan a night out together for fun at least every other week. By economizing and by trading baby-sitting with friends who lived nearby, they could afford such evenings out. When they agreed on what seemed to be workable plans and had written these down in their logs, Pete said: "Good work! You've just succeeded in revising a small part of your working agreement. This could make things a little better for both of you." [Encouraging couples to develop concrete change plans designed to satisfy specific needs, helps to strengthen their sense of movement, intentionality, and hope. It may help them begin to replace mutual hurting cycles with positive, mutual satisfaction cycles.]

When they came for their third session, Pete inquired about how their change plans had worked out. They reported partial success. They had had an evening out together on the weekend. This had been very good. Pete commended them warmly on this step forward. Their plan to have regular times for deeper communicating hadn't materialized. Sue said, "By the time Dickie's asleep, I've *had* it!" They discussed, at length, what they could do about this. Sue added, "There are many things about mothering that are precious to me, but it feels like I'm at it twenty-six hours a day."

After further discussion, Sue asked Jerry if he'd be willing to take care of Dickie for half a day each week, to give her a chance to get out of the house and have a break from full-time mothering. Pete supported her request with the comment: "It seems to me that having a break from parenting to do something creative would be very good for you, Sue. It may be easier to enjoy the times of closeness with Jerry, if you're not so exhausted." Jerry resisted this request tenaciously because of his heavy schedule and expressed anger at being pushed by both Sue and Pete. Pete responded: "I appreciate your openness, Jerry, about feeling pressured. I can understand how you'd feel resentment when we're both pushing you to make a change that would make your heavy schedule even heavier. I guess I was siding with you, Sue, because of my own feelings about the issue." The issue was unresolved at the end of the session, but Jerry's anger, having been dealt with openly, was no longer dominating his feelings. Jerry and Sue agreed to think and talk about the issue and see if they could work out a way to meet both their needs to some extent.

In the next session, there was further discussion of the possible advantages for both of them and for Dickie.

Jerry: It'll take some doing, but, as a dad, I *should* be more involved with Dickie. I'm so wrapped up in my work, we hardly know each other.

Pete: Spending more time with Dickie could have some rewards for you and for him. If you agree to sit with him only because you "should" to relieve Sue, it's not likely to be very satisfying either for you or for him. I find that when I agree to do something only because I should or because of pressure from my wife, I often end up fouling it up or forgetting to do it. [The counselor was attempting to reinforce Jerry's *internal* motivation to make this change.]

In the next session, Pete invited Sue and Jerry to try the "Box and Meadow" exercise (see chapter 2). He explained: "You may find this self-awareness exercise useful in getting in touch with some of your feelings as they relate to your lives together." Pete led them through the experience. Here is a segment of the debriefing that followed.

Jerry: The meadow part was great! I also enjoyed watching the volcano erupt. Wow! But the box part felt like I was shut in a heavy wooden packing crate. That part was a bummer.

Pete: Is that boxed-in feeling familiar?

Jerry (after reflecting for a few moments): I guess I feel shut in by my schedule sometimes.

Sue: And your agreeing to spend more time with Dickie doesn't help things in that department. (Jerry nods in agreement.)

Pete: Jerry, how do you feel about what Sue just said?

Jerry: Good. She's right on target—even though I *want* to spend more time with Dickie.

Pete: I appreciate your awareness of Jerry's feelings, Sue. [By focusing on Sue's sensitivity to Jerry's feelings, Pete was seeking to encourage the development of this kind of empathy by both of them.] Jerry, as you think about your time bind, what do you need to do to free yourself from that boxed-in feeling?

That question led Jerry to focus on a crucial personal growth issue for him–the way he had closed himself in with the self-imposed demand that he complete his graduate program quickly. This issue remained unresolved at the end of the session.

When Sue shared her fantasy experience, she reported that her meadow also was fun, but that her volcano was "scary" and her box "felt like a coffin." Her reflection on the fear of getting close to the erupting volcano gradually helped her see how much frustration-based anger she was holding in. Pete pointed out that this bottled-up, self-directed anger probably was contributing to her continuing depression. When Pete asked her about the coffin, she thought for a few moments.

> **Sue:** My career–it's as if that part of me has been buried.
> **Pete:** It's as if that side of you, the satisfaction of your teaching and getting on with your career, has been put in a coffin. (Sue nodded.) That feels sad to me. What can you do to begin reviving that part of your life, Sue?

She responded that perhaps the free time she'd have, while Jerry took care of Dickie, would help. In the weeks that followed, Sue decided to use her free half day to fulfill a long-time dream–to learn to throw pots. She signed up for a ceramics course at the local junior college. This proved to be a satisfying hobby that helped raise her energy level for coping with the demands of her other roles.

When they evaluated this session, they agreed that some difficult growth issues for both of them had surfaced. Pete affirmed their courage in facing those and recognizing the work required to resolve them growthfully. He added:

> I felt good that you both enjoyed playing in your inner meadows. Your playful sides are still functional, in spite of the pressures in your lives. You might find it good, during your reconnecting times this week, to try "playing in your meadows" together. Give yourselves some pleasure breaks by doing some things together you'd both enjoy. While you're reducing the pain in your lives, why not also increase the pleasure as much as you can?

When they returned for the next session, they reported that they had decided one evening to send out for a pizza to enjoy while they watched their favorite television program together. The sparkle in their eyes communicated how they felt about this pleasure break.

In his individual sessions (which began after the second joint session) Jerry continued to wrestle with his sense of being boxed in by his heavy schedule. This led him to evaluate his intense drive to "get ahead in the academic world" and to look at what it was costing him. After discussing this in several individual and joint sessions, he made a difficult but freeing decision: to postpone the target date for completing the degree for at least another year. This decision opened a larger space in his life for "the things that don't get much emphasis in graduate programs"–planting a small garden, playing his guitar, and spending nonpressured time with his son and with Sue.

Sue's growth work, triggered by the coffin experience, continued in her individual sessions and in the joint sessions. What surfaced was her feelings about the unfairness of their assumption that Dickie was 98 percent her responsibility and that she therefore should indefinitely interrupt her career to care for him. Much of Sue's depression, it later became clear, resulted from the anger she had turned on herself because of her programming as a woman and her guilt about the pregnancy. Her anger stemmed mainly from having her growth options so reduced by the lopsidedness of their marital "contract." It required substantial enhancement of her feelings of self-worth before Sue was willing to push Jerry for basic changes in their working agreement.

At the end of the sixth joint session the three of them evaluated their progress. Sue and Jerry agreed that although things were going somewhat better, they needed to stay in counseling for a while to deal with a variety of unfinished issues. They recontracted with Pete for an additional series of individual and joint growth sessions.

In a subsequent joint session, Jerry reported that he had had a disturbing dream about his father (who had died from a heart attack two years before). Pete invited him to do some growth work with the dream. What emerged was Jerry's unfinished grief about his father's driven life-style and his early death, feelings that had been stirred by Jerry's becoming a father and by his own struggles. In working through these unconscious conflicts about his father and himself, Jerry gained more awareness and freedom in his relationship with Dickie and with the professor who chaired his graduate program (to whom he had been relating as a father substitute). Gradually he began to feel more *present* when he was with Dickie and less inclined to give his power away to his faculty mentor. The fact that Jerry and Sue both did some of their personal growth work, in the presence of the other, proved to be good for their relationship. Experiencing Jerry's dream work, for example, increased Sue's appreciation of her husband's inner struggles with his role as a father. It also triggered her awareness of some of her unfinished growth work in relation to her parents.

To help them explore further the influence of childhood experiences on their present feelings and behavior as spouses and parents, Pete suggested in one session that they try an awareness exercise involving being a child again in their childhood home, in their imagination.[1] This recall experience opened important awareness particularly for Sue. In encountering her "inner parents" she became more aware of the role models she had internalized from observing her parents during her childhood. Her mother had submerged herself totally (with hidden resentment) in her mothering role. She began to see how this old programming had given her a "submissiveness button." When it was pushed it distorted her behavior as a wife and mother. That awareness increased her freedom not to follow this obsolete programming in her current relationships. [The responsiveness of Sue and Jerry to the childhood-home exercise made Pete decide to introduce the Parent-Adult-Child concept from transactions analysis. He presented it as a tool they could use to interrupt their punitive Parent/needy Child cycles of alienation by activating the Adult side of their personalities.]

After the session in which they returned in memory to their childhood homes, Sue continued to reexamine her identity as a woman, her tendency to feel totally responsible for making their relationship work, to avoid owning her own needs even to herself, and to put herself down when she failed to live up to her great mother-great wife image. During this time, Pete encouraged Sue to attend a six-session consciousness-raising growth group for women led by a woman therapist who was on the center's staff. In this group she heard other women describe similar feelings. She began to see how much of her self-esteem problem resulted from her programming as a woman in a sexist society. She felt a warm sense of hope and support for her growth strivings from other women who also were struggling to free themselves from this programming to be full human beings. As a result of this experience, Sue eventually became involved in a group working to challenge and change sexist practices in the schools of their community.

As Sue's consciousness was raised and as her self-esteem grew, she began to use her more self-respecting and assertive side and to attend more to her own needs, not just to the needs of Jerry and Dickie. At times Jerry was bugged by the new, more autonomous and assertive Sue, but he also liked her increased spontaneity and zest for living. Sue's underlying frustration with their lack of plans about when and how she would continue her professional life came into sharp focus during a joint therapy session when Pete invited them to "do some creative dreaming about your future." Pete: "To get a picture of where you want to be a few years from now, close your eyes and imagine that things are the way you'd really like them to be. Be aware of how you feel, how you're spending your time, what your relationship is like, how things have changed." [This exercise is a means of helping people concretize their hopes and mobilize their intentionality.]

This exercise triggered a productive and painful session. In Jerry's "dream", he had finished his graduate program and was well established in a stimulating college teaching job which allowed ample time for enjoying his relationships with Sue and their *three* children. Then Sue described her dream. She had resumed her teaching career and was doing additional graduate work during the summers, to prepare for a school principalship. She said, "I like administration, and I guess I've had a secret yen to have a position in which I could help make things better in a whole school." Her dream also included ample time for enjoying close relationships with Jerry and Dickie, but it didn't include more children.

After both had shared their dreams, Pete asked what they wanted to do about them. Their discussion was heated on the issue of Sue's desire that they set a target date for her to resume teaching and on the issue of having more children. They worked on these crucial areas of conflict during several sessions. Eventually they arrived at a compromise to have one more child when Jerry completed his degree. Pete helped them look at their need to correct the unfairness of their marital contract in the areas of child care and the development of their careers. He supported Jerry by affirming the changes he had made and recognizing his feelings of anger at being pushed by Sue to make even more changes. But Pete also supported Sue's insistence that the basic inequality of their growth opportunities must be corrected, adding: "As you probably know, some couples are working out child care on a shared basis so that the child will know both parents well and so both parents will have a fulfilling life in addition to parenting. I doubt if you'll be able to develop the kind of intimacy you want until you know deep down that your working agreement is fair and equally fulfilling for both of you." After several more sessions of struggle, they worked out a plan that would let Sue continue her teaching the next fall. This involved Jerry's sharing more responsibility for child care and for preparing some of the meals. When the plan eventually was implemented, it helped to relieve their financial pinch as well as to renew Sue's professional development.

After several sessions, in which they had revised parts of their marriage covenant, Pete suggested that they might find it helpful to take an overview of their working agreement. He pointed out that in making their covenant explicit they would have an opportunity to evaluate it and update it in other areas where revisions were needed.[2] He asked each of them to write out, between sessions, their understanding of: what each person expects to give and get from the marriage; the number of children to have; the division of responsibility for earning money, child rearing, doing the necessary "dirty work," making decisions about moving; the division of opportunities for satisfying careers and personal growth; their agreements about friends, relatives, religion and values, time alone, sex, recreation, time to communicate; their plans for revising the agreement periodically; and any other significant aspects of their working agreement. When they took the written statements of their understanding of these issues to the next session, they had a lively time. In general they felt encouraged by discovering how much fairer and growth producing their covenant had become through the changes they had already made. Writing out their understanding of their working-covenant made them aware that there were continuing frustration and conflict in some other areas. They spent several sessions struggling to renegotiate more mutually satisfying agreements in these areas, with much more success in some than in others.

One of the areas on which they concentrated was their love life. They both agreed that their sexual relationship had gradually improved as pent-up anger had decreased, as communication and closeness in other areas of their relationship had increased, and as Sue's self-esteem had grown stronger. Pete observed, "Feeling more connected and fulfilled in your lives generally, seems to be making sex better." When both indicated that they wanted further enrichment in their sex lives, Pete suggested that they might like to try some nondemand pleasuring experiences as homework. Pete recommended and described full-body massage using warm body lotion. He lent them a book on various methods of nondemand pleasuring.[3] When they came to the next session, it was obvious that they had enjoyed this much more than their previous homework assignments.

On the hunch that Dickie's presence might help to make accessible in the counseling process different sides of themselves and their relationship, Pete invited them to bring their son to one session. This proved to be productive as well as enjoyable. Jerry and Sue became aware of some important differences in their feelings and responses to each other when, as Sue said, "our Parent button is pushed."

During another session it came out that Jerry had not told Sue about feeling "really shot down" by critical evaluation of his work as teaching assistant by his major professor several weeks before. Sue confronted Jerry with her hurt that he didn't share his vulnerable feelings with her. This confrontation caused Jerry (after his initial defensiveness subsided) to take a look at how he was trying to maintain a male "success" image in her eyes by hiding his pain when he felt he hadn't measured up to this image. As they shared their feelings about this pattern, it became clear to them that Sue also had had a stake in maintaining him in this image, even though it cut both of them off from the creative closeness that could only come by being vulnerable and open to each other.

As they worked on their plans for the future, Pete offered them an opportunity to use the Time-Values Inventory (see chapter 5), introducing it to them this way:

> The two of you have made important changes in your lives especially in the last few sessions. Your ability to do this is one of the many strengths in your relationship, as I see it. I've noticed that issues of how you use your time keep coming up as you think about changes you're planning. I'd like to suggest that you try this inventory to see if it's useful. It's a simple communication tool to help people focus on how they use their time and what changes they want to make in it. I suggest that you take copies home and set aside a couple of hours to give it a try.

When they returned the next week, they reported that they had gotten "distracted" midway through using the instrument. Awareness of the values implicit in their present use of their time had triggered an extended and at times heated discussion about their hopes for the future. After hearing about their intense sharing, Pete responded (with a grin and tongue in cheek), "Too bad you two got distracted and didn't finish the inventory." The subsequent sessions included further exploration of their long-range growth goals, for themselves and their relationship, and what they needed to do to help each other move toward these. Pete recommended that they maintain the momentum of their growth work by writing out their goals for the next month and the next year in their growth logs, and then use these to work out practical plans together.

One thing that came out of their use of the inventory was a need "to get more going in the spiritual side" of their lives. Jerry said that he was "turned off" by a lot of things about conventional religion but that he also was aware of some needs in this area. They both expressed an interest in exploring ways of satisfying their spiritual needs more fully. Pete encouraged them to tell each other what they found meaningful and what they would like to develop in that side of their lives. They discovered that each had had some moving experiences of wonder and gratitude as they related to

Dickie and sensed that they were keys to the development of this new person. Pete identified these as "peak experiences" and urged them to overcome their shyness about sharing them with each other when they occurred. In response to their need for ways to enrich their spiritual lives, Pete introduced them to some techniques of meditation and imaging (see chapter 4).

In the closing phase of their counseling, Pete invited them to take part in a marriage-enrichment retreat, co-led by Pete and his wife and sponsored by the church that also sponsored the counseling and growth center. On the retreat, Jerry and Sue became well acquainted with Pete's wife and with several couples with whom they "hit it off." They continued to meet informally with a small group of these couples for mutual support and sharing after the retreat. In discussing the retreat with Pete, Sue declared:

> It was fun to be away together in the mountains without Dickie [who stayed with Sue's mother] and with those neat couples! We felt like we were building on things we learned in counseling.
>
> **Jerry added:** Yeah, it was almost worth a sprained ankle in the volleyball game! [By inviting them to attend the couples retreat, Pete was encouraging them to discover the value of periodic intensive growth booster experiences and the importance of having a network of couples who are also committed to nurturing each other's growth.]

After they had been in counseling for about five months, it became clear to Sue and Jerry that their need for Pete's help as a growth facilitator was greatly reduced. Increasingly they were meeting problems in their lives and conflicts in their marriage more constructively and doing their continuing growth work on their own. They discussed this and Pete suggested that they taper off, meeting every other work for several times, before terminating counseling. They spent two of these sessions evaluating where they had come in counseling and firming up growth plans for the future.

In their final evaluation they said that they appreciated Pete's skills and competence but also his humanness and his willingness to share his own feelings, foibles, and personal struggles. They said they felt his respect and his liking of them. Pete responded: "It's been good! It's meant a lot to me to work with you. I appreciate the way you've used counseling for your growth. I've learned some things from your struggles and growth that have been good for me. I guess you know that my door is open if you feel the need for a refresher session." The couple expressed their sadness at leaving.

After their counseling was completed, Pete accepted their invitation to come to their apartment for dinner. Before going he asked if they would like to have a kind of mini-celebration in the form of a "love feast." This turned out to be a meaningful way of expressing their gratitude for the rebirth of their relationship and their commitment to nurture each other's continuing growth. They symbolized all this by an informal ritual that included feeding each other segments of an orange and pieces of bread.

About a year after they finished counseling, Pete invited them to be a "resource couple" in a group of five couples preparing for marriage. The group was co-led by Pete and a social worker on the staff of the center. In this group Sue and Jerry discovered that sharing their continuing struggles and growth openly was very helpful to the younger couples as well as stimulating to their own growth.

A SUMMARY OF THE DYNAMICS AND METHODS USED

(1) *The counselor sought, throughout the counseling, to see and relate to the couple through the growth-hope perspective.* He saw them as persons with many resources for using their crisis as a growth opportunity, and he told them so.

(2) By his attitudes, he let them know that *conflict and anger are normal and continuing ingredients in any close relationships and that these feelings often occur around issues where the growth possibilities are the greatest.* The counselor knew that frustrated dreams and blocked potentializing often get translated into blaming one's marital partner. He knew that when people take responsibility for developing more of their own potentials, the urge to attack, declines. By the end of counseling, the couple were expressing and dealing with their conflicts much more constructively and growthfully.

(3) The counselor *encouraged both individual and relational*

growth, seeing these as potentially complementary. (Spouses sometimes grow apart.) Problems *within* people are intimately interrelated to problems *between* people. The rationale for combining individual and joint growth sessions is to maximize self-support and personal growth on the one hand and mutual growth nurturing on the other. Love grows best when two people are committed to their own and the other's growth.

(4) Throughout the counseling, the counselor *expressed his caring through genuine affirmation,* and encouraged the couple to do the same with each other. Pete assumed that nearly everyone has a self-esteem problem and that sincere affirmation can stimulate growth in self-affirmation. So, he affirmed Sue's and Jerry's latent strengths, their struggles to develop these potentials, and each small, tentative step they took toward a more creative and equal relationship. He sought to affirm their basic worth as persons by his warmth and caring and honesty.

(5) The counselor recognized *the danger of using affirmation in manipulative ways.* He sought to avoid this by expressing affirmation only when he really felt it. He tried to avoid *using* affirmation as a technique, since to do so is inherently manipulative and destructive of the authenticity of the counseling relationship. Furthermore, he sought to be aware of his own tendency to be manipulative in relationships so that he could choose not to be seduced by this temptation.

(6) *The counselor sought to balance and integrate caring affirmation with caring confrontation.* Confrontation became increasingly prominent as the trust and hope level of the relationship increased. By his firm, gentle confrontation the counselor was saying implicitly: "Speaking openly about the way I see you limiting your growth is an expression of my respect and caring for you as persons. It's an invitation for you to examine and change these things, if you decide these are changes you desire. The fact that I'm not afraid to confront you honestly is an affirmation of the strength I see in you to accept and use or to reject what I say."

(7) *Intentionality was used throughout the counseling as a key working concept.* Pete believed and told the couple that they possessed the freedom to initiate significant changes in their individual lives and in their marriage, if they chose. He assumed that this

freedom was limited, to some degree, by past choices and experiences but that the freedom and power to choose increase as the power is exercised constructively.

(8) The counselor aimed at *awakening and nurturing realistic hope for creative change* in the couple. He did this by employing all the approaches described above and by coaching the couple in developing and implementing action plans that enabled them to discover that they *could*, in fact, intentionally change their lives and their relationship. Pete's knowledge that they could change helped them maintain hope during times when they felt "bogged down" in their conflict and resistance to change.

(9) The counselor sought to *help them tap the energy of joy and pleasure*, in the midst of their pain, conflict, and struggle. In the conflict-free area of their relationship, it was possible for them to enjoy each other and to use these experiences to motivate and energize growth in areas of conflict.

(10) *The emphasis throughout was on living more fully and zestfully in the present and on moving by choice toward a better future.* The past was dealt with in this counseling only when it was found to be an interference with or a neglected resource for living fully in the present.

(11) The counselor assumed that *complementary growth can occur through counseling in both the area of feelings* and the area of *behavior*. Working through old oppressive attitudes and feelings can facilitate changes in behavior. Sue and Jerry discovered that their feelings of self-esteem, hope, competence, and mutual enjoyment increased as they learned new behavioral skills that were more responsive to each other's needs. Conversely, growth in the area of feelings helped to energize and motivate constructive changes in their behavior.

(12) The counseling illustrates the *usefulness of the developmental perspective*. The counselor's understanding of the problems of Jerry and Sue was enhanced by his knowledge of the nature and dynamics of developmental crises that are typical of young adults in our culture. He also tried to be aware of the unique aspects of the crisis of these particular young adults and to avoid the temptation to use the developmental perspective as a Procrustean bed into which all young adults must be made to fit.

(13) The counselor was aware of the ways in which *social problems such as sexist attitudes and practices provide a context within which individual and relational problems tend to flourish.* He helped the couple discover how their traditional programming as a woman and as a man was impoverishing their relationship and contributing to their problems. The counselor helped them recontract so that their love would be based on a strong foundation of equality and justice. He encouraged Sue's consciousness-raising and her growing sense of autonomy and strength. He helped Jerry affirm and develop his nurturing, caring, vulnerable side and to relax his exorbitant demands on himself as a man.

(14) The counselor encouraged the couple *to deal explicitly with value and spiritual issues.* He viewed value issues as pivotal to their growth because their values guided their choices and therefore determined the directions of change. In addition to the value-reformulation exercise, a basic revision of their priorities and values was implicit in the whole counseling process. Pete viewed the developing spiritual lives of Jerry and Sue as sources of energy for creative change. Before the sessions, Pete often practiced the discipline of "spiritual centering," getting in touch with the center of loving energy within his consciousness and then visualizing the couple and surrounding them with this healing energy.

(15) The counselor encouraged them *to learn how to draw on the resources of a wider community of nurture and support.* He knew that continuing growth can be facilitated by sharing one's life and growth with other growing persons in a supportive community of mutual growth.

(16) The relationship between Pete and the couple was increasingly egalitarian and nonhierarchical. At the outset, the couple had Pete on a pedestal as "the authority" who would help them. As trust and mutuality grew in the relationship, and as Pete shared his humanness with them, the one-up role in which they had perceived him gradually changed. At the end of the counseling they could perceive him more accurately (including his faults) and relate to him as a trusted friend.

Chapter 4

Spiritual Growth–The Key to All Wholeness

People attempt to overcome the threat of nonbeing by denying the self. The outcome of this is ironic: that which is dreaded triumphs, for we are caught in the self-contradictory bind of shrinking our being to avoid nonbeing. The only alternative is self-actualization in spite of the ever-present nothingness.

–Mary Daly, *Beyond God the Father* (Boston: Beacon Press, 1973), p. 23.

The human needs a framework of values, a philosophy of life ... to live by and understand by, in about the same sense that he needs sunlight, calcium, or love.

–Abraham Maslow, *Toward a Psychology of Being* (New York: Van Nostrand, 1968), pp. xx, iv, 206.

Spiritual growth is the key to all human growth. Because human beings are inherently transpersonal and transcendent, there is no way to "fulfill" oneself except in relationship to the larger spiritual reality. By experiencing an intimate growing relationship with this reality, we connect with the Source of all growth and creativity. Spiritual growth work aims at liberating the "vertical dimension" of our lives. It seeks to liberate our belief systems, our values, and our relationship with God so that our lives will become more open to these deep wellsprings of healing and growth. We human beings are creatures who live in our hopes and meanings and in our beliefs about what is ultimately real and significant. These aspects of our lives have a profound influence on the quality of our self-identity and on the quality of our relationships with people, nature, institutions, and God. If our religion is growth-stimulating, it will diminish our flowering in other areas. If our religion is growth-stimulating, it can open the doors of our whole being to the nurturing energies of a living universe.

Our deepest growth need is to develop our transcendent potentialities, our spiritual selves. Our basic alienation is from this central core of our being.[1] Our "spiritual" strivings and needs are not, as some psychotherapeutic schools have suggested, derivative from, and only mirrors of other more basic aspects of our personality. Instead they are central in everything that is *human* about us human beings!

Wholeness Counseling takes a radically nonreductionistic view of the universal religious strivings of humankind. This is in harmony with the thinking of persons like Carl Jung, Abraham Maslow, and Roberto Assagioli. This approach does not ignore Freud's insights about the ways in which our early-life experiences and unconscious drives often distort our ability to perceive and experience spiritual reality. Freud's insights have important implications for the practical task of facilitating spiritual growth. The goal of such work is to help people experience spiritual reality clearly, in the here and now, with minimal blurring from infantile longings and unfinished growth needs. The assumption of those psychotherapies that view the "spiritual" as derivative from other needs is that religious and value issues will be automatically resolved if psychological and interpersonal difficulties are resolved. Growth Counseling recognizes the interdependency of all dimensions of human beings but affirms that changes in the spiritual-valuing dimension are often primary and essential in freeing persons to change in other areas.

FACILITATING SPIRITUAL GROWTH

As a way of getting into the dynamics of spiritual growth, let's examine one session (in condensed form) with Henry R., a lawyer in his mid-thirties. When he came to this session it was obvious from his fear-filled eyes as well as from his verbal report that he was feeling flooded by anxiety. His answers to my initial questions showed that he was unaware of what might be causing his feelings although he suspected they were related to the recent death of his dad. Henry had used the Gestalt Therapy "empty chair" method on several occasions. When I asked if he would like to try to resolve his anxiety by this approach, he agreed. What follows is a condensed version of the full session.

I asked Henry to face an empty chair, close his eyes, stay with his feelings, and imagine that someone was sitting in the chair. After a few moments, I asked him who was there. He replied that it was his mother (who had been an alcoholic).

> **Howard:** How old are you?
> **Henry:** Nine.
> **Howard:** What do you want to say to your mother?
> **Henry:** Nothing.
> **Howard:** What's happening?
> **Henry:** I've just thrown a biscuit at my mother and hit her on the breast. I'm angry!

I invited him to express his feelings to her.

> **Henry shouted:** You bitch. Why don't you fix my breakfast?
> **Howard:** Now sit in the other chair and be your mother.
> **Mother:** Now you've done it. You've hurt me. (in an angry whining voice) Someday I'll die, and then you'll be sorry. (She did die a few years later.)

Henry moved back to his own chair and sank into what seemed to be a heavy silence.

> **Howard:** What's happening now?
> **Henry:** I'm running upstairs and hiding behind the curtain in my bedroom.
> **Howard:** Who are you hiding from?
> **Henry:** From God.

I invited Henry to put God into the empty chair and to talk to him. He hesitated, and when he spoke his voice quavered as he expressed a torrent of fear and guilt. Then, at my invitation he moved to the other chair.

> **God's voice** (angrily): You're a terrible person! You've done it! You hurt your mother and you're going to get it!
> **Henry** (pleadingly): I didn't mean to do it! I'm sorry! I'm sorry! (begins to sob)

This interchange between Henry and "God" continued for a while. Then Henry relaxed.

> **Howard:** What are you experiencing now?
> **Henry:** It's not really God in the chair, it's my old man. It was his voice that was accusing me.

I asked Henry if he wanted to say anything to his father, who was now in the empty chair. He expressed angry resentment to his father for defending his mother's neglect. When this intense anger was drained off, Henry moved to his father's chair and spoke for him in a soft, sad voice: "I really love you, son, and I'm sorry I take her side when you're the one being neglected by her in her drunken stupors. I should be there when you need me. I want to hold you and love you." (Henry's body relaxed noticeably.)

Later he put his mother back in the empty chair and expressed his fears of being deserted by her. Henry then responded for her, expressing feeling hopelessly trapped in her drinking and not knowing how to be the loving mother she wanted to be: "I'm so tied up in my dismal problems. I can't give you what you need from me, my love. And I'm sorry." Henry's body sagged. He began to weep quietly.

> **Howard** (after Henry's crying stopped): What are you experiencing now?
> **Henry:** My shaking's gone. I feel quiet and light inside.

We then spent considerable time debriefing his experience. Henry saw how he had absolutized his father's threats by putting them on "God." He became aware of how he was frightening himself by this inner "demon" he had created from his experiences with his angry father and, it developed later, his rejecting mother. During this session he had "exorcised" his demon thereby defusing his guilt and his terror that "God will kill me because I killed my mom." Relinquishing the idolatry with which he had distorted his perception of reality was a profound experience of spiritual growth for him. At the close of the session, I invited him to phone me after he had shared his experience with his wife, Sally. My intention was to encourage him to talk it through with her and to give him an immediate opportunity to share with me whatever happened in that crucial relationship. When he called, he reported that the conversation with Sally had been very helpful. His willingness to be vulnerable during the counseling session by entering deeply into his fears and expressing his anguish in tears seemed to free him to risk being vulnerable with Sally. Such vulnerability, which was difficult for Henry as for most men in our culture, opens the door to growth in close relationships.

This session was a breakthrough for Henry in his ongoing growth work. His growth moved much faster in the sessions that followed. In a joint session with the couple, Sally described how their relationship had opened up. Later I commented to Henry that he was projecting much less of his past into his current relationships. He replied that he had "let go of a lot of that old garbage during the God session."

Exorcising the "demon" with which he was terrifying himself and blocking his own growth enabled Henry to deal with his inner parents as finite human beings and eventually, as he put it, "to lay them to rest, at last!" After letting go of the demonized ghosts of his parents, he reported having significantly more energy for his work, for his important relationships, and for enjoying life. Predictably, his spiritual life became more energized after he let go of his demon. It took him several months of intensive growth work in counseling to consolidate the growth he had begun in that key session, but that session was the turning point in his self-liberation. His breakthrough enabled him to sustain and actualize hope of changing in the midst of his continuing growth struggles.

WHAT IS SPIRITUAL GROWTH?

The spiritual dimension of our lives consists of the ways in which we satisfy seven interrelated spiritual needs: the need for a *viable philosophy* of life, for *creative values*, for a *relationship with a loving God*, for *developing our higher self*, for a sense of *trustful belonging in the universe*, for renewing *moments of transcendence*, and for a *caring community* that nurtures spiritual growth. These needs are present in all persons including those most secularized in their thought and most alienated from institutionalized religions. They are existential needs in the sense that they are inherent in human existence. Psychoanalyst Erich Fromm observes: "Because the need for a system of orientation and devotion is an intrinsic part of human existence, we can understand the intensity of this need. Indeed, there is *no other more powerful source of energy* in man [sic]."[2]

The satisfaction of those needs is essential for robust mental, physical, and spiritual health. The goal of spiritual growth work is learning how to satisfy the basic spiritual needs in growthful ways. What constitutes growthful satisfaction varies tremendously among and within cultures. In many cultures, including our own, the majority of people still seek to satisfy their spiritual needs in organized religions. But, as societies like ours become increasingly secularized, more and more people focus their spiritual search outside religious institutions. Unless religious institutions change drastically, and become more effective *spiritual growth centers*, alienation from them will become epidemic. (In this discussion, I am using the term *religious* in its broad sense to include the variety of ways in which people satisfy their spiritual needs.)

Many people do not satisfy their spiritual needs in healthy ways. This retards their growth and impoverishes their lives and significant relationships. Many others satisfy their spiritual needs in ways that expand and enrich their lives and relationships. Our personal religion can be crippling or creative, entrapping or liberating of our potential. Our religion can be a *weight* on our spirit or *wings* by which we soar. *Salugenic* (health- and growth-producing) *religion* results when people satisfy their spiritual needs in open, life-affirming, reality-respecting ways. *Pathogenic* (sickness-producing, growth-blocking) *religion* results when people attempt (unsuccessfully) to satisfy their needs in idolatrous, rigid, authoritarian, life-constricting, and reality-denying ways.[3]

Here are some criteria for identifying salugenic religion. I have found these useful in facilitating spiritual growth in counseling sessions and growth groups. *Do the religious beliefs, attitudes, and practices of persons*

- give them a meaningful philosophy of life that provides trust and hope in face of the inevitable tragedies of life?
- provide creative values and ethical sensitivities that serve as inner guidelines for behavior that is both personally and socially responsible?
- provide an integrating, energizing, growing relationship with that loving spirit that religions call God?
- nurture the transcendent dimensions of persons' lives, their higher Self?
- inspire an ecological love of nature and a reverence for all life?
- provide for a regular renewal of basic trust by affirming a deep sense of belonging in the universe?
- bring the inner enrichment and growth that comes from "peak experiences"?
- offer the person a growth-enabling community of caring?
- build bridges rather than barriers between them and persons with differing values and faith systems?
- enhance love and self-acceptance (rather than fear and guilt) in their inner life?
- foster self-esteem and the "owning" of their strengths?
- stimulate the growth of their inner freedom and autonomy?
- help them develop depth relationships committed to mutual growth?
- encourage the vital energies of sex and assertiveness to be used in affirmative, responsible ways rather than in repressive or people-damaging ways?
- foster realistic hope by encouraging the acceptance rather than the denial of reality?
- provide them with effective means of moving from the alienation of appropriate guilt to healing reconciliation with themselves, other persons, and God?
- encourage creative change in their beliefs and values to keep these congruent with their intellectual growth?

–provide effective means of keeping in touch with the creative resources of the unconscious through living symbols, meaningful rituals, and vital myths?

–encourage them to keep in touch with both the soft, vulnerable, nurturing, receptive, feelingful side *and* the assertive, rational, intentional, ethically demanding side of their personalities?

–make them aware of person-hurting institutional practices and motivate them to work to change these forces that oppress potentializing on a massive scale?

–give them the trust, hope, and meaning to face their awareness of death and the inevitable losses of life and to allow their awareness to make living more precious?

–keep them aware of the basic wonder and mystery of all life and growth?

–encourage heightened aliveness and joy and celebration of the *good gift of life?*

All these criteria refer to different facets of one reality–the spiritual wholeness of persons. The criteria are stated broadly so that they can be applied to the spiritual dimensions of any individual's life, whatever her or his religious beliefs or affiliations.

How can these criteria for salugenic religion be used in facilitating growth work in counseling and teaching? I find it helpful to hold the criteria *loosely* in the back of my mind, to help identify those areas of religious beliefs or practices (my own and my clients') in which spiritual growth is needed. The list of criteria can be discussed in growth groups as a communication exercise to enhance awareness in the area of spiritual wholeness. Most people have a wealth of latent spiritual capacities that can be developed. If they continue to grow spiritually their personal religion becomes an increasing source of hope and energy for coping with crises growthfully. The criteria also can be used to increase the sensitivity of counselors and group leaders to the potential for more growth-enabling spirituality in their clients. Because of their experiences with clients, many counselors and therapists (like Freud) are keenly aware of the prevalence of pathogenic, growth-blocking religion but have little understanding of creative, salugenic religion.

The spiritual dimensions of our lives are inextricably interrelated with all other aspects of our personalities and our relationships, in a circular fashion. Pathogenic religion both reflects and reinforces impoverished, nonactualizing personality dynamics and relationships. Conversely, salugenic religion both reflects and enhances the growth of persons in other areas of their lives.

TRANSFORMING EXISTENTIAL ANXIETY

Understanding the power of our spiritual needs and the importance of satisfying them growthfully requires that we examine the existential anxiety and loneliness that are a part of our basic human awareness. Anxiety is the response to anything that we perceive as a fundamental threat to our well-being. Neurotic anxiety stems from inner conflicts and from the threat that repressed impulses will escape into conscious awareness. In contrast, *existential anxiety* is nonpathological, normal anxiety. It stems from human self-awareness. We are the animals who know we will die! On some level we are all aware of the awesome, inescapable fact that we are living-dying creatures. Death as an eventual certainty is, consciously or unconsciously, a constant awareness in our lives. How we deny or face this awareness influences profoundly the depth, creativity, and aliveness of our personalities.

As human beings we are trapped by our rootage in nature. We are all subject to the forces of aging, sickness, pain, and death. We lack what Big Daddy, in Tennessee Williams' play *Cat on a Hot Tin Roof* calls the "pig's advantage"–ignorance of our mortality. The nature of existential anxiety has been discussed by many thinkers including Sören Kierkegaard, Simone de Beauvoir, Erich Fromm, Paul Tillich, Erik Erikson, Rollo May, Ernest Becker, and Mary Daly. Erikson calls it the "ego chill." Tillich described it as our "heritage of finitude."

Unlike neurotic anxiety, there are no psychological or psychotherapeutic answers to existential anxiety. There are only philosophical or religious answers. Existential anxiety is inherent in our very existence as self-aware creatures. But its influence on us can be either crippling and deadening or creative and enlivening, a stimulus or a barrier to hope and growth, depending on how we respond to it.

In our death-denying culture, there are countless ways of seeking to avoid the painful awareness of our mortality. As Karen Horney suggested, neurosis is a way of avoiding one's fear of death by avoiding being fully alive. If I keep myself half dead by guilt, compulsive work, unawareness, and worry, death is less threatening, for I have little to lose. Mary Daly has suggested (in the quotation with which I began this chapter) that the denial of the self in religion is an attempt to escape the threat of nonbeing by denying our being. Many addictions are attempts to escape from existential anxiety by centering life around a false absolute, by making a god of alcohol, food, work, drugs, sex, money, or success. In this sense, addictions are forms of psychological idolatry. They are attempts to meet spiritual needs by nonspiritual means. The problem with all these defenses against awareness of death is that they ultimately make the fear of death more devastating. All idols eventually betray their worshipers.[4]

Our fearful attitudes toward death make our bodies up-tight and rob us of aliveness and spontaneity. It is as though we were trying to stop time by not feeling, experiencing, and enjoying life, by rationing our life energy and not living fully. Feminist therapist Anne Kent Rush declares:

> Paradoxically this course, instead of prolonging life, by keeping our bodies rigid, trying to stop time, . . . quickly brings death into the present. When I set myself in this frame of mind I miss the vitality of my present; I remain in a conceptual state—once removed from reality. . . . If I can let myself move, flow, open up and evolve, rather than trying to stop time at one "young" age, then death could be another phase on the continuum.[5]

In *Journey to Ixtlan*, the Indian don Juan points out to Carlos Castaneda that he is wasting one of his greatest powers by his hopeless, fearful feelings toward death. Don Juan declares: "Death is your eternal companion. It is always to our left, at an arm's length. Death is the only wise advisor that we have." Elisabeth Kübler-Ross has arrived at a similar insight: "It is the denial of death that is partially responsible for people living empty, purposeless lives. . . . Only when we understand the real meaning of death to human existence will we have the courage to become what we are destined to be."[6]

I lived with a chronic fear of death after my sister died when I was four. During my mid-years', awareness of a rapidly contracting future stirred up waves of existential anxiety. One of the most liberating effects of my experience of enlivening (described in the first chapter) was a striking reduction of my fear of aging and death. The truth that I had known in my head for years is now more real in my heart: *The answer to the fear of death is the experience of really being alive now!* When I let myself feel my aliveness in the here-and-now, death loses its spooky awesomeness. I become aware of my involvement in the ongoingness of life. I now understand the words of a client at the end of her growth-oriented therapy: "When I came for therapy I thought I was afraid of dying, but it turned out I was really afraid of living." Our defenses against awareness of dying diminish our aliveness and thus make dying more threatening.

All this points to the key role of salugenic religion in self-actualization. The only effective way of coping creatively with existential anxiety is to risk coming alive now. But this requires existential hope and courage, the courage to be and to become. This courage can come only from an awareness of the ultimate trustworthiness of existence. Salugenic religion is the source of this awareness. By the satisfaction of our deep spiritual hungers, growthful religion provides the existential courage to be and to become, freely and joyfully. Out of the ancient wisdom of the East, Lao Tsu declared: "A man of outward courage dares to die; a man of inward courage dares to live."[7]

After heart surgery and his brush with death, an insightful minister declared: "I think the basic aim of religion, really, is to conquer fear–the fear of living intensely and fully–and to release us to believe in life, to believe in one another, and to believe in ourselves."[8] By experiencing a warm sense of God's love, the ego chill of existential anxiety is transformed into motivation and energy to create, to live fully and joyfully, to pour out energies into the ongoingness of the human story. If our spiritual experience frees us to live fully, death will lose much of its power to frighten us. In the experience of basic trust and aliveness, existential anxiety is transformed into what Sören Kierkegaard called "a school"–that is, a growth experience. It becomes the energy that motivates and empowers human creativity!

OUR PLANET'S SPIRITUAL CRISIS

Humankind is in the midst of a profound spiritual crisis that makes it difficult to satisfy our spiritual hungers growthfully. Behind the widespread participation in organized religion in America, there is hope-vacuum rooted in a profoundly materialistic, irreligious world view which is reflected in our thing-worshipping lifestyles. The dimension of transcendence as an energizing force has largely disappeared from the lives of millions of people in Western societies, leaving them in a flat, two-dimensional world. This has resulted from many factors. Central among these is the dizzy speed of social change that has produced a massive breakdown of traditional belief and value systems. These systems of meaning, and the rituals and myths that supported them, were the primary ways by which human beings met their spiritual needs and handled existential anxiety through the centuries. Millions of people today are questioning and openly rejecting the old authority-centered ways of deciding what is good and ultimately true. Old comfortable ways of believing and valuing are no longer acceptable or satisfying to countless people. But many have not yet developed new, more creative ways. We are in a period of mind-boggling, spirit-numbing change, an anxiety-saturated time of spiritual transition. The impact of this spiritual crisis is felt unconsciously by every person and in every close relationship. The dim awareness of this crisis is one factor that brings people to counseling. Moreover, it influences the counselor and everything that happens in counseling in subtle but profound ways.

The spiritual vacuum of our times has produced an epidemic of spiritual pathologies. Psychiatrist Robert Jay Lifton describes our spiritual dilemma:

> In times of relative equilibrium, a society's symbols and institutions provide comforting guidelines for inner experiences as well as external behavior. But in times of severe historical dislocation, these institutions and symbols–whether having to

do with worship, work, learning, punishment, or pleasure–lose their power and psychological legitimacy. We still live in them, but they no longer live in us.[9]

No matter how hard we try, many of us cannot conjure up "fresh faith in old dreams." As a people in transition we walk a lonely path.

The collapse of authority-centered belief and value systems is made more anxiety-producing by the loneliness of our mobile technological society. Millions of people feel uprooted and nameless, cut off from the nurture of belonging to a community of caring persons. When "Roots" was first shown, 80 million Americans clung to their television sets watching it, dimly aware of the pain of their personal and spiritual rootlessness. The personal loneliness that results from the loss of community exposes us to a deeper *existential loneliness*–the awareness we usually ignore, that we *are* ultimately alone in our own inner experiences. We build communication bridges to other consciousnesses, but in all the ultimate experiences (such as dying) we are *alone*. Persons who suffer from a deeply impoverished sense of basic trust and belonging feel utterly alone in the universe. The spiritual vacuum of our times has left many people exposed to tidal waves of existential loneliness and anxiety. They feel frozen by the "ego chill."

Reactionary backlashes in religion and politics are negative responses to our spiritual crisis; they are what Erich Fromm called "escapes from freedom." Anxious, spiritually impoverished people retreat into "true believer" solutions, proclaimed passionately by messianic authority figures who know how to exploit the anxieties of our age for their own power. In the long run, such simplistic "solutions" to complex human issues leave their devotees with disillusionment and greater despair.

When seen from the growth perspective, our global spiritual crisis is an unprecedented *opportunity for spiritual growth*. That so many of us no longer find ready-made, believable answers from religious institutions and authority figures, makes it necessary to think and decide for ourselves. This new freedom is frightening. Letting go of our comfortable answers forces us to struggle to "work out [our] own salvation with fear and trembling," as the

New Testament puts it (Phil. 2:12). We are challenged, perhaps as never before in human history, to discover beliefs that really make sense *to us*. We are called to develop constructive, self-validating ethical guidelines to which we can commit ourselves wholeheartedly. The resources of our religious heritages are now just that–*resources* for testing and using in our own struggles to find what is meaningful in our lives. The contemporary spiritual crisis, which is reflected in so many of the dilemmas that send people to counselors, is a magnificent challenge to humankind–a challenge to *grow up* ethically and spiritually.

Our society's crisis has produced an enormous surge of spiritual searching.[10] A new world view that makes a place for a reality that goes beyond the limited "reality" of materialism is desperately needed and seems to be emerging gradually in our times. Such a view makes a central place for a *spiritual* reality that is ultimately more real and abiding than the space-time world.

The flat, two-dimensional "reality" of materialism is bleak and sterile as a conceptual environment for human growth. Reclaiming the "vertical dimension" as our very essence is crucial to full human potentializing. Learning to experience and enjoy the Spirit which is at the heart of reality, in oneself and in one's relationships with others and with nature, is to become aware of the sacred, the "beyond within" ourselves and all of life. Let's look now at some ways in which spiritual growth can occur.

AN ENLIVENING PHILOSOPHY OF LIFE

A viable belief system concerning the purpose of existence helps provide a foundation of meaning and hope for a person's life. The conviction that one's existence has a purpose, in spite of the inevitable tragedies of life, equips one to live more fully in the midst of those tragedies. Studies in prisoner of war camps have shown that human beings can bear enormous stress if there is meaning for them in the situation. Hope in a meaningful future is a central motivation for growth. But to be sustained, hope must be grounded in what the individual perceives as ultimately real. A sense that life has a larger spiritual meaning keeps hope alive in what would otherwise be a hopeless situation. As feminist philosopher Mary Daly points out, all authentic human hope is ontological in the sense that it requires facing nothingness through the transforming power of living faith.[11]

What are some ways of helping people revitalize their assumptions about the meaningfulness of their lives? In crisis counseling and in grief recovery groups it is sometimes helpful to ask "opening questions," questions that invite people to open the spiritual dimension of their lives to reflection and increased awareness. Here are examples of such questions: What have you learned about life from this painful experience? How does this crisis you've been going through relate to your personal faith? Are your religious beliefs a help in handling this rough situation? Do you see anything constructive resulting from coping with this loss? Does all this seem to have any meaning as you understand things? These questions should be asked only after the person is coming out of the crisis or loss. When people are invited to reflect on their crises or losses, they often become aware of spiritual resources within themselves and in their relationship on which they can draw to discover meaning in what has happened.

The following communication exercise, devised for use in marriage-enrichment events to encourage couples to share their spiritual struggles and growth, can also be used in counseling, therapy, and growth groups to focus on meaning-to-life issues. The exercise consists of giving persons opportunity to complete the following sentences in writing and then to explore fully the feelings and issues that emerge:

> "My life has the most (least) meaning, hope, and energy when–"
> "The values that are exciting and really worth living for are–"
> "I feel most alive (hopeful; like celebrating the goodness of life) when–"
> "The beliefs that I now affirm as true and important are–"
> "The beliefs from my childhood religion that no longer make sense to me are–"
> "The parts of my faith that enrich my relationship (help me handle losses) are–"
> "The way I really feel about the church is–"

"To strengthen and deepen my spiritual life, I need to–"
"The way I feel about discussing these questions is–"

Growth-enabling counseling and therapy must involve respect for the clients' own beliefs and values, their right to choose the direction of their own spiritual pilgrimage. But, the counselor's philosophy of life, working values, and spiritual vitality can be important resources in the spiritual struggles of clients. The level of healing energy in counseling relationships is profoundly affected by the life orientation and spiritual aliveness of the counselor. If we experience life as meaningful in some basic sense, if we have some grounding for our hope in that which we see as ultimately real, if our belief and value systems are authentic and life affirming, our clients will experience these in a variety of subtle ways and be helped thereby. When clients are saying no to themselves and to life, it is tremendously healing to develop a relationship of mutual trust and caring with a person who is saying yes to life because life has said yes to her or him. Therefore, tending to our own continuing spiritual growth as counselors and therapists is essential if we are to be spiritual growth enablers for others.

THE NEED FOR CREATIVE VALUES

Abraham Maslow was convinced that the value-life of human beings is biologically rooted. There seemed to him to be a species-wide need (comparable to the need for basic food elements and vitamins) for what he called "B" (for being) values–e.g., truth, goodness, beauty, wholeness, justice, playfulness, meaningfulness, etc. These values are biological necessities for avoiding illness and for achieving one's full potential. The epidemic of spiritual illnesses ("metapathologies") resulting from deprivation of these values include anomie, alienation, meaninglessness, loss of zest for life, hopelessness, boredom, and axiological depression.[12] As feminist theologians and therapists are making clear, the human potentialities whose widespread neglect in our male-dominated culture threaten the very survival of humankind are those most valued and developed by women: nurturing intimate relationships; nurturing growth in the young; sensitivity and responsiveness to feelings; cooperation and collaboration; vulnerability and compassion. These values must be added to Maslow's "B" values as essential for resolving the value crisis of our times.[13]

When one is aware of the crucial importance of values to wholeness, the role of impoverished values in all manner of personal and interpersonal problems becomes clear. One's working values are the inner guidelines on the basis of which countless decisions that determine the direction of one's life are made every day. Chronic problems in living always reflect distorted or impoverished values in need of revision. Personal crises often confront us with profound value issues. A man's mid-years heart attack, for example, can confront him with the need to change the patriarchal values—the overvaluing of money, achievement, getting ahead at any price—that fed the compulsive striving leading to the heart attack.

I have described a variety of methods of value renewal and spiritual renewal elsewhere.[14] Value-reformulation exercises are useful in individual, couple, and group counseling. They provide a structured opportunity to critique one's life-investment plan and to decide if the values and priorities implicit in the plan need revising to let one's life and intimate relationships be more fulfilling, growth nurturing, and constructive to society. Here are some questions you can use to discover if your values are contributing to wholeness in yourself, your relationships, and in society: I suggest that you take time to reflect on each question, considering what changes in your values are needed.

Do my values and the life-style they produce allow me time

 –to maintain robust physical, mental, and spiritual health?
 –to develop my intellectual, spiritual, and creative potential?
 –to do the fulfilling, important, and exciting things I want to do?
 –to love, nurture, and enjoy the people I really care about (including myself)?
 –to invest myself in significant, challenging, self-transcending causes that will help make my community a place of growth for everyone?
 –to contribute to the survival and potentializing of the whole human family on a livable planet?

At the end of chapter 5 there is a values-reformulation instrument for use in applying these criteria.

AN ENERGIZING RELATION WITH GOD

The heart of spiritual growth-work is opening oneself more fully to the vital energy which is the creative Spirit of the universe. Opening one's life to this spiritual energy helps fill one's inner being with warmth and zest for using well the gift of each day. The most common barriers to increased spiritual vitality are the hard inner lumps of obsolete beliefs, unfaced doubts, and false absolutes, the shoddy gods we unwittingly worship. Eliminating these logjams in one's inner stream allows the spiritual energies of the universe to flow again. Dialoguing with one's spiritual barriers (as Henry did with his "demon") is an effective tool for clearing away growth-blocking religious feelings, attitudes, and beliefs and thus facilitating spiritual growth.

There are a variety of spiritual disciplines that can help people develop a more open, dynamic relationship with God's enlivening Spirit. Meditation and meditative imaging, in my experience, are the most valuable of these disciplines. Used together, they can help meet several spiritual needs, in addition to deepening our relationship with God. They can strengthen our awareness of our at-homeness in the whole creation, provide nurture for one's higher Self, and open one to peak experiences. Learning to meditate and use guided imaging can deepen and enrich our own lives as counselors which inevitably enhances our relations with clients. Learning and practicing these simple disciplines also can help equip us to teach meditative and imaging techniques to clients and students in therapy classes and growth groups.

Roberto Assagioli, founder of psychosynthesis, saw the values and the potential of meditation as part of therapy: "Meditation helps the patient to an expanded consciousness . . . in a completely natural way. The course of therapy is shorter with meditation. . . . Meditation has a good chance of eventually becoming one of the leading therapeutic techniques."[15]

There are numerous meditative techniques that can be integrated in growth-oriented counseling, therapy, and education. In its most basic form meditation is any method of centering one's awareness, of focusing and quieting one's consciousness, and thus getting in touch with what is happening in one's body and in the deeper self to which most people seldom attend. Many meditative techniques are simply ways of temporarily interrupting the busy flow of thoughts, images, and feelings in our consciousness and thus entering a "serenity zone" within us. Letting one's mental motor idle for even ten minutes each day can be deeply renewing in itself. When one is in such a clear, quiet, uncluttered consciousness, the use of guided images can open one to further spiritual awareness and renewing energy. Persons in various religious traditions have held that meditation is a way of enriching one's prayer experience by entering the deeper dimensions of the self in which one encounters Spirit. At the close of this chapter I'll lead you through a two-phase meditative exercise that combines meditative centering and guided imaging.

Scientific studies of various meditative and relaxation techniques, reported in Herbert Benson's *Relaxation Response*, show that they tend to produce psychological and spiritual benefits as well as physiological improvement such as decreased blood pressure and muscle tension.[16] Benson's book brings together recent scientific findings on meditation with ancient methods of meditation from the East and the West. He describes a simple four-step way to experience the "relaxation response" (pp. 114-115). It seems clear from his findings that the various methods such as TM, Zen, yoga, and autogenic training have much in common and that most people do not require an expensive course to learn how to meditate effectively.

In addition to Benson's book, here are some resources that are useful for teaching yourself meditative and imaging methods: Lawrence LeShan's *How to Meditate* includes guidelines for integrating meditation and psychotherapy. Morton T. Kelsey's *The Other Side of Silence* is a guide to Christian meditation. William Johnson's *Silent Music, The Science of Meditation* relates meditation to healing and intimacy. Carolyn Stahl's *Opening to God* gives guidelines for using biblical imagery in meditation and describes thirty such meditative experiences.[17]

Experiencing and valuing the "feminine" in divinity–the warm, nurturing rebirthing side of Spirit–and integrating this with the cognitive, ethical side persons have tended to over-develop can enrich one's spiritual life tremendously. Five centuries before the Christian era, the sage Lao Tsu affirmed the importance of spiritual wholeness for creativity: "One who has a man's wings and a woman's also is in himself a womb of the world, and being a womb of the world, continuously, endlessly gives birth."[18] In the next chapter I will explore the rich resources provided by feminist theologians who are helping us develop the "wings" of women's spiritual heritage.

NURTURING THE SPIRITUAL SELF

For many of us, spiritual growth requires discovering and allowing to become central in our lives what psychosynthesis calls our "higher Self." (In traditional religious language this was called the soul.) Centering our growth on our higher Self can help us experience the transformation of our existential loneliness. To the degree that we stay in touch with our higher Self, this dimension of ourselves will energize our relationships with people and give us an ontological transcending basis for self-worth.

As a client in a session with a therapist trained in psychosynthesis, I had been struggling futilely to resolve some hard lumps of grief and anger within me. For a variety of reasons, I was getting nowhere in my attempts to liberate myself from these. The turning point came when the therapist invited me to get in touch with my higher Self–"the place within you where you are whole and together"–and to see the issues with which I had been struggling from that perspective. When I did this, the cold lumps seemed to melt. My depression and sense of entrapment lifted as I felt a flow of energy within.

RENEWING A SENSE OF BELONGING

Basic trust is revitalized in persons by their awareness of belonging to, of being at home in, the universe. An alcoholic with whom I once counseled expressed the existential loneliness that comes from a lack of such belongingness. He said, "Howard, I feel like an orphan in the universe." Teilhard de Chardin describes the depth of our relatedness to the universe in words that I find very moving:

> The human soul, however independently created our philosophy represents it as being, is inseparable, in birth and growth, from the universe into which it is born. In each soul, God loves and partly saves the whole world which that soul sums up in an incommunicable and particular way. But this summing up, this welding, are not given to us ready made and complete. . . . It is we who, through our activities, must industriously assemble the widely scattered elements. The labour of seaweed as it concentrates in its tissues the substances scattered, in infinitesimal qualities, throughout the vast layers of ocean, the industry of bees as they make honey from the juices broadcast in so many flowers–these are but pale images of the ceaseless working-over that all the forces of the universe undergo in us in order to reach the level of spirit.[19]

Our organic interrelatedness is with the whole biosphere. With the dawning of human personality, a new dimension of reality emerged within the biosphere–the reality of the network of minds and spirits (which Teilhard de Chardin calls the "noosphere"). Within our own minds and spirits we can be nurtured by our connections with other minds and with the creative, loving Spirit of the universe. The methods of deepening one's sense of at-homeness in the universe are essentially the same as those of nurturing awareness of the higher Self and energizing one's relation with Spirit.

INCREASING AWARENESS OF PEAK EXPERIENCES

Peak experiences, as Abraham Maslow described them, are "the best moments of human being . . . the happiest moments of life, . . . experiences of ecstasy, rapture, bliss, of the greatest joy."[20] He saw these little mystical moments as experiences of self-actualization which are life-validating in that they make life worthwhile and heal the splits within and among persons and between the person and the world. Peak experiences can occur often in the process of potentializing if we become aware of the profound mystery and wonder in *all* growth. Precious moments of transcendence, according to Roberto Assagioli, can be actively fostered through the use of methods he calls "spiritual psychosynthesis." But they also are potentially available in many everyday experiences. Spiritual dullness makes it easy to miss peak experiences.

As I awoke the morning I wrote this, I experienced a brief moment of transcendence. (I was writing at a cabin in the mountains.) I caught a glimpse through my bedroom window of the sun on the pine trees, I breathed the fresh morning air and was aware for that moment of the wonder of simply being alive. Surprisingly all this happened in spite of feelings, in another part of my mind, of heaviness from some difficult problems I was facing.

Toward the end of his life, Maslow became aware of "high plateau experiences" which are ongoing rather than climactic. Plateau experiences are a kind of unitive consciousness, a simultaneous perception of the sacred and the ordinary, or, better, the sacred *in* the ordinary. He observes (somewhat whimsically, I suspect): "I have noticed that it's possible to sit and look at something miraculous for an hour and enjoy every second of it. On the other hand, you can't have an hour-long orgasm."[21] Unlike mystical peaks, plateau experiences can be cognitive. Maslow saw that knowledge can be positively rather than negatively correlated with a sense of reverence, awe, humility, mystery, and ultimate ignorance. Plateau experiences occur when one lives with a sense of inner illumination, with an awareness of the preciousness, beauty, and poignancy of ordinary things. Peak and high plateau experiences are times of opening oneself to receiving the energy of growth and healing that is at the heart of the universe, of reawakening one's sense of at-homeness in the universe.

A COMMUNITY OF CARING AND NURTURE

Spiritual growth occurs most readily in a group committed to spiritual values. This can take place in a two-person group, like a deep friendship or creative marriage. It can be in a small spiritual growth group of persons committed to nurturing ethical and spiritual discovery (like Alcoholics Anonymous). It can be in a church or a synagogue where there is both that warm caring and refreshing openness that allows the growth formula to come alive in relationship. As counselors we should find or develop and encourage our clients to find or develop a spirit-nurturing community of caring within which they can experience their deep bond with humankind and the universe.

An illuminating study of why churches are losing members, revealed that the key is the failure of people to nurture and support one another. Those who were closely identified with a congregation felt cared about in warm human relationships there. Those who had become inactive had done so primarily because they lacked feelings of being cared about.[22] It is in communities of mutual caring that the fullest development of spiritual potentials takes place.

RENEWING YOUR SPIRITUAL ENERGIES

Here is a meditative-imaging exercise I use to help myself and my clients renew spiritual energies. I invite you to try it now. Read the instructions until you come to the slash (/). Then close your eyes and do what is suggested. Take as long as you wish.

Find a quiet place where you can be uninterrupted for the next fifteen minutes, a place where you can feel at home with yourself. / While standing, tense and relax all your muscles several times. Stretch and wiggle any part of your body that feels tight. / Sit in a chair with your lower spine straight. / Close your eyes and be aware of your breathing. Allow any tension within you to flow out as you exhale. / Focus only on the inflow and outflow of the air through your nostrils, repeating the word *One* with each exhalation. / Continue to do this until your breathing quiets. Yield to experiencing your breathing in the here and now. / If a thought, image, sound, or an itch enters your consciousness don't try to get rid of it. Just release it and let it recede as you keep focusing on your breathing and continue to repeat *One* over and over. / Do this until the spaces between your breaths lengthen and you feel clear and quiet within. /

Now, picture yourself walking on a gently rising path up a mountain. / As you walk repeat the word *Up* each time you exhale. Feel the lift of your spirit as you ascend. / When you reach the top, be aware of being in the presence of a Source of warmth and wisdom. Visualize this spiritual reality as a soft, warm, healing light. / Let yourself enjoy this spiritual energy. Let it gradually fill you and surround you with healing power. Continue this until you feel energized and cleansed and renewed. / Become aware that this healing light is really a part of you, a wonderful part, your higher Self, the Spirit in the center of your being. /

Now picture a person you care about deeply. / See that person surrounded with the warm, healing light. Let it nurture and energize that person for several moments. Picture others you care about, one at a time—your family, friends, clients, persons in special need, the poor and oppressed in other countries and your own. Surround each of them with the healing light. / Continue to feel yourself bathed and filled with the spiritual energy as you send energy to others. / When you are finished receiving and sending energy, decide what you will do to celebrate your experience. For example, let yourself be a graceful bird. Enjoy soaring above the mountaintop in the warm energy. / When you're ready, see yourself coming down the mountain path to your everyday life in the valley. / See yourself the way you'd like to be in your activities today—confident, healed, strong, creative, etc. / Surround yourself and your activities and the relationships that you'll probably have today with energy from the mountaintop. / During the day, be aware of any changes in your relationship, your values, your uses of time, resulting from your experience on the mountain.

Don't be discouraged if this exercise isn't very meaningful the first time. I recommend that you use it each day for a week to see if it becomes more meaningful as you gain experience with this approach. You may decide to experiment with different focus words in the first part—e.g., *Peace, Yes, Warm, Shalom*. Find the one that helps you focus and quiet your consciousness. Or experiment with other symbols on the mountaintop—an opening rose; a wise, loving person; or a living symbol from your religious tradition. The use of the technique of symbolic ascent in guided imagery is, according to psychosynthesis therapist Robert Gerard, a way of reaching higher levels of consciousness. He reports: "It has been found empirically that imagined upward movement, particularly the theme of climbing a mountain and up in the sky, tends to transform . . . feelings, and may even generate mystical experiences of cosmic light and love. . . . Repeated experiences of this nature open the channel to higher consciousness."[23]

Chapter 5

Biblical and Theological Resources for Wholeness Counseling

> People who are trained in a religious tradition as well as the procedures of psychotherapy do have access to a large source of wisdom, the wisdom gathered through the centuries by men and women reflecting on their experiences of God.
>
> –Ann Belford Ulanov, "The Place of Religion in the Training of Pastoral Counselors," *Journal of Religion and Health*, vol. 15 (1976), p. 8.

The growth approach to people has been around for a long time. A concern for healing and wholeness appears in some form in many of humankind's major religious traditions.[1] For persons whose spiritual roots are in the Jewish-Christian traditions, it's good to know that many aspects of the growth approach are indigenous to those ancient spiritual heritages.

In spite of my enthusiasm for the usefulness of biblical insights for potentializing, this chapter proved to be a difficult and challenging portion of the book for me to write. Both personally and professionally, my life has been rooted in the Judeo-Christian traditions. Probing these tradition, from the growth perspective, makes me painfully aware of the negative impact of the patriarchal orientation of the traditions on the growth of women and also of men. It is clear to me that the integration of the insights from the heritage of women's spirituality into our traditions is crucial if they are to become wellsprings of wholeness for women and men.

In this chapter I'll share some biblical images and insights that I have found useful as resources for spiritual growth work. I won't do an exegetical study or a depth exploration of the growth-oriented biblical passages. Instead I will give an overview of biblical growth insights that have come alive for me in my personal life and in my work. I will then suggest some ways in which the traditional growth thrust can be enriched by incorporating images and insights from ancient and contemporary spiritual discoveries of women.

There are at least three reasons why knowledge of the biblical springs of the growth approach can be useful: First, this time-tested wisdom provides valuable resources for energizing and guiding spiritual growth. I hope that this chapter will encourage you to use insights from an enriched biblical heritage, integrated with your own spiritual discoveries, as resources for enabling whole-person growth. Second, the biblical wisdom about the nature and process of human becoming can help to correct and deepen contemporary psychosocial understandings of growth. If one brings the biblical growth thrust into dialogue with insights from these current sources, each perspective can enrich the other, thereby creating a synthesis of the best in each for the service of whole-person growth. Third, understanding the biblical as well as the contemporary growth thrusts allows one to describe both sources when offering growth programs in various settings. In my experience, some people in churches respond with less anxiety and more willingness to participate when they become aware of the grounding of growth programs in their religious traditions. Secular-minded people often are turned off by "religious" language.

BIBLICAL GROWTH IMAGES

Growth images appear throughout the Bible. To allow some of these to speak to you, read the following passages, stopping after each one to close your eyes and picture what is described. Interact with the image, and be open to its message for you:

> [A good person is] like a tree
>   planted by streams of water,
> that yields its fruit in its season,
>   and its leaf does not wither. (Ps. 1:3)

The winter is past. . . .
The flowers appear on the earth,
　the time of singing has come,
and the voice of the turtledove
　is heard in our land.
The fig tree puts forth its figs,
　and the vines are in blossom;
　　they give forth fragrance. (Song of Sol. 2:11-13)

For waters shall break forth in the wilderness,
　and streams in the desert;
the burning sand shall become a pool,
　and the thirsty ground springs of water; . . .
　the grass shall become reeds and rushes. (Isa. 35:6-7)

[In describing the new era of wholeness, caring, and justice, Jesus said,]

Consider the lilies of the field, how they grow. (Matt. 6:28)

"The kingdom of heaven is like a grain of mustard seed which a man took and sowed in his field; it is the smallest of all seeds, but when it has grown it is the greatest of shrubs." (Matt. 13:31-32)

"The kingdom of heaven is like leaven which a woman took and hid in three measures of flour, till it was all leavened." (Matt. 13:33)

"A sower went out to sow. . . . Some seeds fell along the path. . . . Other seeds fell upon thorns. . . . Other seeds fell on good soil and brought forth grain, some a hundredfold, some sixty, some thirty." (Matt. 13:3-8)

"Whoever does not receive the kingdom of God like a child shall not enter it." And he took them in his arms and blessed them, laying his hands upon them. (Mark 10:15-16)

He who supplies seed to the sower and bread for food will supply and multiply your resources. (II Cor. 9:10)

BIBLICAL AFFIRMATIONS OF HUMAN POTENTIALS

Our rich potentialities are affirmed in the biblical record when human beings are described as being created "little less than God"

(Ps. 8:5). The startling assertion in the first creation story (see Gen. 1:27) that we are made in the image of God is a ringing affirmation of the mysterious, wonderful possibilities within all human beings. John Calvin declared in his commentary on Genesis that the creation of human beings in the divine image is "a remarkable instance of divine goodness which can never be sufficiently proclaimed."[2] Human growth, as I understand it, is the continuing process of fulfilling the image of the highest within us by the unfolding of our capacities for full personhood. It is important to remember that in the anthropology of the Jewish Bible, the whole person was seen as created in the divine image, not just one's spirit or mind.[3] It is by developing our potentialities for wholeness–physically, psychologically, relationally, spiritually–that the divine image comes into its unique expression in us. Thus we participate in the wonderful variety of the creative process by which God's living presence is expressed in the world. (Unfortunately, some have missed the divine image idea to justify species narcissism and cruel treatment of other animals.)

Liberation is a continuing motif through the Bible. The essence of liberation is freedom to be and to become all that one has the God-given capacity to become. Here are some liberation themes from the New Testament: "We are not children of the slave but of the free woman. . . . Stand fast therefore, and do not submit again to a yoke of slavery" (Gal. 4:31-5:1). "You will know the truth, and the truth will make you free" (John 8:32). Reading from Isaiah in his hometown synagogue, Jesus used his Hebrew scripture to describe his mission: "He hath sent me to proclaim release to the captives and recovering of sight to the blind, to set at liberty those who are oppressed" (Luke 4:18). Liberation is release *from* everything that oppresses or blocks human becoming; it is *toward* the fulfillment of our unique, God-intended personhood.

In the biblical view, all growth is a gift of the Creator of life. Our remarkable potentials are good gifts to be accepted and developed through the unfolding gift of growth. We receive the emerging gift as we develop our distinctively human capacities–our potential for caring and compassion, for creativity and self-transcendence, for heightened awareness and expanding consciousness, for constructive conscience and depth communication with others and with that "creative-responsive love"[4] which is God. Hope is a persistent motif throughout the Bible, hope derived from experiencing this energizing Love. Our hope for the future is grounded in this ultimate Source of life and growth. We are invited to rejoice in this hope. (See Rom. 12:12.)

We are never alone in our struggles to grow. The gravitational pull of the spiritual universe supports and energizes our becoming. In mysterious but utterly dependable ways, the fulfillment of our growth is empowered by the creative Spirit which is within us and at the heart of all reality. With appropriate excitement the writer of Romans declared, "The whole creation is on tiptoe to see the wonderful sight of the sons of God coming into their own" (Rom. 8:19 Phillips). This affirmation would have been completed and its power increased tremendously if (as in Acts 2:17) the *daughters* of God also were included explicitly.

Awareness of the gift quality of growth can be wonderfully freeing. It can help liberate us from the heavy feeling that growth depends entirely on our own efforts, on our own skills and cleverness. Fortunately, we cannot and need not create either the capacity for growth or the inner drive that motivates growth. These are *there* in us as a gift of Life. The Spirit within us lures and energizes us to take part in the creative process of self/other potentializing. As growth-oriented counselors, our task is to help people learn to open themselves to the natural, God-given process of becoming and thus to accelerate growth. There's a healthy perspective in Paul's words: "I planted, Apollos watered, but God gave the growth" (I Cor. 3:6). It's humbling and reassuring to remember that the people with whom we work in counseling, therapy, and teaching, sometimes grow in spite of rather than because of what we do.

THE GOALS OF GROWTH

In the most lyrical of the Gospels, Jesus' purpose in coming is described as being so that people could have "life . . . in all its fullness" (John 10:10 NEB). What a beautiful statement of the goal of growth work! Life in all its fullness means "wholeness centered in spirit."[5] Christians believe that Jesus Christ shows us in the flesh what life in all its fullness means. Humans meet in him a love-filled, growing person, so fully alive that those who touched him experienced healing and growth. In him we encounter that unfolding wholeness that God intends for all persons. The person-centered values embodied in Jesus' life and relationships reflect the heart of spiritual reality. These values (which have many affinities with what Maslow called "Being values") are trustworthy guideposts on the path to greater wholeness.

From a Christian perspective, Jesus the "word became flesh." God is no longer to be sought "out there" alienated from our human beingness. Spiritual growth happens in us as we discover and develop the inner authority of spirit-centered aliveness. It was this inner authority that gave Jesus the energy and power to challenge outmoded patterns of spirituality and to identify fully with the poor, the disinherited, the powerless and oppressed in his society.[6]

Jesus' amazing aliveness for Christians somehow transcends time. It can still be experienced as a healing growth-enabling energy. Paul Tillich called this reality the "new being." Experiencing this transforming reality is linked, in Tillich's thought, with continuing spiritual growth (called "sanctification" in traditional theological language).[7] "Growing into the full stature of Christ" (see Eph. 4:12) means participating in the new being by developing one's own unique expression of "life in all its fullness." It means seeking to live as true to our unique potentials as Jesus was to his.

Jesus' way of relating to people was remarkably growth-facilitating. His deep sensitivity and caring made his relationships with all kinds of people–including the poor, the sick, sinners, and prostitutes–I-Thou encounters which facilitated their continuing growth and his. "Ordinary" people responded in extraordinary, growthful ways. The response of women to Jesus makes it clear that he saw and related to them, not as inferior or as the property of men (as they were regarded generally in that patriarchial time) but as full human beings, with the same rich, God-given potential as men. In all four Gospels a woman, Mary Magdala, is the primary witness of the death, burial, and resurrection of Jesus. "She was sent to the disciples to proclaim the Easter kergyma . . . Bernard of Clairvaux correctly called her 'apostle to the apostles.'"[8]

The renaming of Simon Bar-jona (see Matt. 16:18) is another dramatic illustration of the impact of Jesus' way of perceiving people. Jesus must have seen in him enormous potential for leadership and strength of which Simon was not yet aware. Jesus said to him, in effect: "Simon, my friend, I'm going to give you a new name. I'm going to call you Peter (which means "rock") to help you see what you can become." The fact that Jesus saw the hidden core of potential strength within him must have encouraged Peter to discover this strength. By affirming what Peter could become, Jesus helped him to become. Jesus' hope and expectations helped Peter develop his rich potentialities. After a dramatic illustration of his weakness (the triple denials), Peter's growth allowed him to become a dynamic leader in the first-century church.

THE PROCESS OF GROWTH

Some of the richest growth images of the New Testament refer to the way the new, transformed era of wholeness–the kingdom of God–is coming. (The hierarchical term *kingdom* is used in a radically new, liberated way in the Gospels.) This new era is coming by a process of growth–like a sprouting mustard seed, like leaven in bread dough, like seeds planted in a variety of soils, like talents invested carefully so as to yield maximum return (see Matt. 25:14-30). Through this process of growth, a new spirit is developing in human consciousness, relationships, and community. Implicit in these growth parables is an invitation to each of us to participate in the exciting process by which this new quality of human existence is coming into being within and among us. As in all potentializing, we are called to cooperate with the Creator of life and thus play a small but significant part as co-creators of new life for humankind.

The beautiful Hebrew word *shalom* describes both the goal and the setting within which growth toward wholeness occurs. The word means "sound, healthy, or whole" (as well as "peace, hello, good-bye").[9] It is in a shalom community that mutual transformation and growth occur most readily. The purpose of the church is to become a shalom community, a place of mutual growth where "hearts may be encouraged as they are knit together in love" (Col. 2:2). When churches are true to their calling (which many are not) they are spirit-centered communities, drawn together by a joyful commitment to mutual caring and growth and to their mission of growth to the world.

A shalom community is drawn together by one Spirit into an organic unity–one body (see I Cor. 12:12). Facilitating wholeness is a shared and reciprocal responsibility. Each person has her or his unique growth gifts and growth calling which only that person can fulfill. In such a caring community, the growth formula–"speaking the truth in love" (Eph. 4:15)–becomes an experienced reality. The growth élan is liberated when grace, the love one does not have to earn, and judgment, a confrontation with that part of reality one is ignoring to one's own and others' hurt, are experienced together in human relationships. Experiencing the growth formula in a shalom community empowers one to reach out growthfully to others. Thus the shalom community becomes a channel through which the energy of God's love and justice move to respond to the needs of the world.

A crucial biblical insight is that growth pursued for its own sake, without regard for others' growth, becomes a cul de sac. Growth is understood as essentially relational. To paraphrase (very freely) the words attributed to Jesus in Matthew 16:25, a person who hoards her or his life will miss life in all its fullness. The secret of continuing growth is to invest yourself in relationships of mutual growth. This relational-outreach emphasis is a healthy corrective to the self-centered hyperindividualism that sometimes appears in psychotherapeutic thought and within the human potentials movement.

In the biblical heritage there is an integrating sense of our interrelatedness with the whole community of humankind. The parameters of our concern for liberation and growth encompass the whole human family with whom we are deeply and inextricably related. In this tradition there is also a deep sense of the goodness of all creation and our organic ties with all living things. Here are the roots of whole-earth conscience and caring–an ecological consciousness. As Corita Kent and Joseph Pintauró put it well: "To believe in God is to build a bridge between yourself and everything worth being one with."[10]

RESISTANCE TO GROWTH

There is a realistic awareness in the Bible of the depth of our estrangement from our potentials, of our agonizing alienation from ourselves, one another, and nature. There is also a conviction that somehow all this is rooted in our alienation from God's healing, life-giving love. The myth of the Fall in Genesis 3 is powerful, poetic statement of humankind's alienation from the image of God which is our potential. The biblical view of sin is much more realistic than some contemporary humanists have been about human evil and the powerful, persistent resistances to wholeness in individuals, close relationships, institutions, and history. The open-eyed realism can be a healthy corrective to the sunny optimism regarding human growth that one sometimes encounters in the human potentials movement.

Biblical writers were acutely aware of the destructiveness of severely diminished wholeness. The belief in demon possession can be dismissed as a naïve first-century misconception of mental illness as caused by the invasion of evil forces into the personality. But there certainly is "demonic" destructiveness in the profound self-alienation and blocked growth of a person suffering from a condition like paranoia. The contemporary understanding of paranoia holds that such persons are unable to accept their hostile and sexual impulses as real parts of themselves. They project these rejected aspects of themselves onto others, perceiving those persons as dangerous or evil. The suspicious, hostile behavior of paranoid persons (stemming from their distorted perceptions) invites the very responses from others they fear—rejection and hostility. The vicious cycle of increasing self-other alienation in the paranoid person becomes truly "demonic" in its malignant destructiveness and in the extreme difficulties involved in interrupting the cycle.

Recent studies of paranoia in women, minority persons, and the elderly illuminate the ways in which the real rejection and oppression by society become intertwined with and reinforce illusory rejection and oppression in the minds of such persons. Sexism, racism, and ageism are the societal context which feeds the vicious cycle of self-other alienation. The findings of these studies parallel the awareness of the eighth-century (B.C.E.) prophets that sin is both individual and collective, that growth-crippling forces are in our social institutions as well as within ourselves and in our close relationships.

The biblical insight about the "iniquity of the fathers" (Ex. 34:7) is an ancient parallel to current understanding of the way growth-limiting patterns are transmitted in the social organism of a family. Conjoint family therapists have offered convincing evidence that neurotic, growth-blocking communication patterns are learned by children from their parents and thus transmitted from generation to generation through family interaction.

For reasons discussed in chapter 2, I cannot accept classical theology's interpretation of the Fall as a symbol of some deep flaw in our "natures" that inevitably and irreparably sabotages our wholeness. But one cannot ignore the grim fact that blocked growth and interpersonal destructiveness flourish in our world. As Don Browning has observed, an overoptimistic self-understanding of human beings poses real dangers in our situation. If we overestimate human benevolence and underestimate the reality of evil, we will be unable to see or cope constructively with our human destructiveness.[11] The most viable approach to this complex issue, as I now see it, is to hold in tension and keep in dialogue the biblical view and most optimistic psychological views. Each holds vital elements of the truth that can free us from self-other oppression.

GROWTH AS STRUGGLE, DEATH, AND REBIRTH

The biblical heritage makes it clear that, although the potential for growth is a gift, it requires intentionality, struggle, and often pain to actualize this gift. Images of the narrow gate and straight way (see Matt. 7:14), of taking up one's cross (see Matt. 16:24), of dying and being born anew (see John 3:3; Rom. 6:6), all communicate this awareness. Ultimately growth is wonderfully freeing and rewarding, but the process of letting go of our comfortable growth-blocking defenses often is difficult and painful. The first step of growth may be to experience the "dark night of the soul." Frequently it requires a descent into the abyss of self-confrontation and despair about our phoney emptiness to crack our defensive shell and open us to the need for radical change. Such a positive surrender can open us to others and to the gift of growth. The journey toward liberation is often, as Kunkel wrote for me in his book, *down* before it is up.

A couple comes to counseling with a mutually destructive, deadening marriage. They are killing each other, creatively and spiritually (and often physically, as well) by starving each other's heart hungers. The first essential step toward the rebirth of their relationship is to face the agonizing deadness of their way of relating. If they learn how to nurture rather than starve their love, their distancing defenses gradually will die, and they can rebuild their relationship on a more just, mutually fulfilling contract. As this occurs, they will move from "death" to the birth of new life within and between themselves.

The New Testament image of resurrection is a ringing affirmation of the possibility of new, authentic, human existence.[12] But the process of growing toward this new quality of life often is like a series of deaths and rebirths. The pain, struggle, and eventual joy of the death-rebirth process is caught by these words attributed to Jesus: "You will be sorrowful, but your sorrow will turn into joy. When a woman is in travail, she has sorrow . . . ; but when she is delivered of the child, she no longer remembers the anguish, for joy that a child is born into the world" (John 16:20-21).

The powerful *resistances* to growth are seen, in the biblical heritage, in the context of the more powerful *resources* for growth. Sin is viewed in the wider context of salvation, despair in the context of hope, dying in the context of resurrection, judgment in the context of grace. Seeing the darkness of the human self-other alienation in the context of Light, somehow transforms the darkness.

One meaning of the biblical word for *salvation* is "to heal and make whole." The New Testament declaration (see Rom. 3:21) that salvation is by grace through faith is an insight that can be experienced and validated in growth-enabling counseling and therapy. By the time they come for help, most people have reached near despair on their works-righteousness treadmill. Years of futile scrambling to try to earn feelings of acceptance from others, years of forcing themselves to be "good" in the conventional sense, years of attempting to please others by conforming–all this becomes increasingly discouraging and exhausting. This works-righteousness orientation breeds perfectionism: "If I only do things more perfectly, then perhaps I'll feel accepted." It also breeds guilt, anger, and depression–guilt because one can never measure up to the exaggerated oughts, anger because one is missing really living, depression when anger is directed at oneself as punishment for the guilt. In effective counseling, the dawning of trust (faith) in the counselor and faint, new hope in the possibility of change allows such persons to risk opening themselves to experience accepting love (grace) which does not have to be deserved or earned. Hearing a warm affirming yes from another allows them gradually to say a tentative yes to themselves. We can say an authentic yes to another only to the extent that we have heard a yes (in our own therapy, growth struggles, or spiritual experience) and have responded by saying yes to ourselves. Fortunately even our partial, fractured yes can help some people hear the growth-empowering yes of their higher Self. For those of us who have been entrapped in the workaholic treadmill, experiencing acceptance we do not have to earn is like a breath of fresh air on a sultry, smoggy day. It awakens hope and releases energy for change by the dawning awareness that we *are* accepted as persons of irreducible worth.

How does this view of the path toward wholeness relate to the biblical recognition that potentializing takes place through a series of intentional choices and actions, guided by our values? How does this ethical dimension of growth relate to the experience of depth acceptance just described? It is clear that only as we confront and change the person-hurting values that misguide our choices and actions will growth become possible. The inner transformation of experienced grace can produce profound changes in one's conscience, close relationships, and behavior. There is movement from a rigid, authoritarian conscience toward a more open, autonomous conscience that is "a call to . . . full humanity."[13] As this occurs, responsible behavior flows not from the guilt and fear-producing "oughts" and "shoulds" of society but from a spontaneous positive response to the unfolding gift of inner growth toward wholeness. Ethical decisions still may be complex and difficult, but the motivation for making them is gratitude and responsive love flowing from one's experience of depth acceptance.

The experience of inner transformation also helps liberate one's relation with time. The importance of living fully in the precious here-and-now moment, an emphasis in contemporary growth approaches, has its biblical antecedent: "This is the day the Lord has made; rejoice and be glad in it" (Ps. 118:24). Our experience of the present can be deepened and enriched by the past and the future.

The central problems that prevent our using the past as a resource in the present are guilt and idolatry (of the past). The biblical growth resource for transforming guilt is reconciling forgiveness. It is noteworthy that the word *salvation* as used in the Gospel stories of healing has a double meaning—being reconciled and being made whole. A close link is seen between the spiritual healing of reconciling forgiveness and the restoration of wholeness to the body. The problems that keep us from using the future creatively are anxiety and hopelessness. The resources for transforming these are trust and hope grounded in experiencing God's nurturing maternal love. The eschatological thrust in the New Testament is a clear statement that our future, as well as our past and present, is an arena of God's healing, growthing love. Hope is our response to the call of Spirit to a new future.

TOWARD A WHOLE THEOLOGY

As a man trained in male-oriented theology, I sometimes have trouble hearing what feminist theologians of liberation are saying. But when I am able to listen (out of my awareness of my own spiritual hungers and the lack of "food" in much traditional theology), my energy level rises. I become aware of insights and images that complement, correct, and enrich the tradition in which I was trained. These insights and images, I am convinced, are essential resources for deepening the spiritual roots of Wholeness Counseling. To integrate the best in the biblical tradition with contributions from the new feminist spirituality is crucial for the full potentializing of both women and men.

Most theology, through the centuries, reflects the spiritual experiences of men. The biblical images and understandings of God represent, for the most part, the reflection and inspiration of men. There is evidence that the spiritual experiences and insights of women have been largely excluded by the men who shaped the development of the scriptures and theology of the Judeo-Christian heritage through the centuries. As theologian Nelle Morton declares:

> Any theology developed by one sex, out of the experience of one sex, and taught predominantly by one sex cannot possibly

be lived out of as if it were whole theology. For whole theology is possible only when the whole people become part of its process, and that includes women. And in time, wholeness may be approximated when men can begin to hear women . . . and when men and women together can participate fully and equally in bringing faith to expression.[14]

Through the centuries the very same religious tradition that promises "life in all its fullness" for all persons has been misused to impose growth-limiting constrictions on half the human family, in the name of God. The patriarchal images, beliefs, and values often have been used to limit rather than liberate the full becoming of women and also of men. There has been an "unholy alliance" between religion and sexism.[15]

The second creation story (see Gen. 2-3) is one of many examples of the way religion and sexism have reinforced each other. In the traditional male interpretations of that male story, Eve is seen as created as an afterthought to the creation of Adam. She is derived from a part of him (a significant male-serving reversal of normal birth) to be a helper of the man. The male interpreters likewise pictured Eve as a seductive temptress and used her as a scapegoat to account for the origin of human suffering and death. As early as 1854, Sarah Josepha Hale rejected these male interpretations of the Genesis stories, pointing out that woman was the *last* work in the ascending scale of creation and therefore must be best in those finer qualities that raise human beings above the animals.[16] The interpretations of Hale and other women scholars who followed her have been largely ignored by male theologians and church leaders. Through the centuries, male interpretations of this story have been used to keep women in their "God-ordained" place as inferior servants of men and as dangerous temptresses who threaten to corrupt the purer rationality and spirituality of men. There are numerous other biblical passages that also have been used to maintain the privileges and power of men in family, church, and society. Patriarchal theology is a vivid example of a central thesis of liberation theologies–that theological images and understandings tend to maintain the privileges of the power elite in the societies that created the theologies.

Those who value the Judeo-Christian tradition can free the resources of that tradition to be used in more growth-enabling ways by doing several things. The first is to stop misusing the Bible to justify treating women as less than full persons of equal value with men. To do this requires that the male biases that appear in many biblical statements about women-men relations be seen for what they are–the assumptions of the patriarchal society within which the Bible came into being. To illustrate, many Christians take the injunction in Ephesians 5:22-24 to be a statement of eternal truth about wife-husband relationships. This passage, when so understood, pressures wives to be "subject in everything to their husbands." To misunderstand and misuse the Bible in this way diminishes growth for both sexes and blocks the growth potentials of marriage. To confuse the Bible's precious wisdom about life and relationships with statements reflecting the patriarchal context of its origins is biblical malpractice!

Second, the resources of our tradition can be used more growthfully by lifting and implementing the vision of liberation for *all* persons which, in spite of the patriarchal influence, is in the Bible. The affirmation of human equality, freedom, and unity in Galatians 3:28 is a powerful expression of this freeing vision. To say that in Christ Jesus there is "neither male nor female" is to recognize that, in terms of what is basically real and important, it is our *humanity*, not our gender, that matters. To the degree that this vision of equality is really implemented in women-men relationships, in the church, and other social institutions, the painful alienation of the sexes will be healed. Unfortunately, implementation of the vision has yet to occur in most of our society's institutions. Elisabeth Schussler Fiorenza observes:

> The failure of the church to realize the vision of Galatians 3:28-29 in its own institution and praxis has as consequence a long sexist theology of the church which attempts to justify the ecclesial praxis of inequality and to suppress the Christian vision and call to freedom and equality within the church.[17]

To implement this vision in the church would involve liberating the language, liturgies, leadership, theologies, and structures of churches from the institutional pathology of sexism.

The third thing that can be done to use our tradition in liberating ways is to recognize, prize, and build on the surviving remnants of the earlier heritage of women's spirituality that still remain in the Bible. Biblical scholar Phylis Trible has contributed significantly to this recovery process in her book *God and the Rhetoric of Sexuality*. At the close of that volume she reflects on the results of her study:

> Clearly, the patriarchal stamp of scripture is permanent. But just as clearly, interpretation of its contents is forever changing. . . . Moving across cultures and centuries, then, the Bible informed a feminist perspective, and correspondingly, a feminist perspective enlightened the Bible . . . this interaction results in new interpretations of old texts; moreover, it uncovered neglected traditions to reveal countervoices within a patriarchal document . . . the Bible is a potential witness against *all* our interpretations. . . .
> "What woman, having ten silver coins, if she loses one coin, does not light a lamp and sweep the house and seek diligently until she finds it?" My search has also been for the lost tokens of faith–for the remnant that makes the difference. Now at the end of this search I join the ancient woman who, having found the lost coin, "called together her friends and neighbors saying, 'Rejoice with me, for I have found the coin that I had lost.'" (Luke 15:9)[18]

Many of the images of growth described earlier in this chapter–trees and water, flowers, spring and rebirth–are probably fragments of the rich ancient tradition of feminine spirituality that survived the rise of patriarchal religion. There are numerous other biblical remnants of this tradition. Second Isaiah includes this affirmation of God's maternal, growth-enabling care:

> "As one whom his mother comforts,
>   so I will comfort you. . . .
> You shall see, and your heart shall rejoice;
>   your bones shall flourish like the grass" (Isa. 66:13-14).

Perhaps the biblical images and insights from women's ancient spiritual search, taken together, can become a nucleus around which the spiritual heritage of women, which was largely repressed and lost during the centuries of patriarchy, can be reclaimed as a vital resource for the spiritual liberation and growth both of women and of men.

The fourth thing that Christians can do is recognize and emulate the liberating wholeness of Jesus, who integrated those qualities most often identified with men–strength, courage, forcefulness, leadership, concern for justice–and the qualities most often identified with women–compassion, caring, tenderness, and responsiveness to the deep needs of others.[19] He showed by his full humanity that these qualities are neither masculine nor feminine but *human* possibilities that belong together in whole persons. Although he called God Father (reflecting his times), many of the attributes of deity in his teachings are those associated most often (in his culture and ours) with mothers–tender love, mercy, nurture, compassion.

Jesus' liberated attitudes and relationships with women could well be emulated today. He refused to conform to his sexist culture's efforts to constrict women to domestic servant roles, as illustrated in the story of Mary and Martha (see Mark 10:2 ff). In a heavily patriarchal culture that considered it improper to teach women sacred truths, Jesus treated women with the same respect as he did men, freely sharing with them his new understanding of spiritual reality. As a remarkably whole growing human being, Jesus' dynamic life can be a source of energy-for-growth.

The fifth thing that can be done to help liberate our use of the tradition is to open our minds to learn from feminist theologians, both Jewish and Christian. Immersing oneself in writings such as these can put one in touch with a stream of confronting, growth-enabling insights: Nelle Morton's *The Journey Is Home*; Judith Plaskow and Carol Christi, (Eds.), *Weaving the Visions, New Patterns in Feminist Spirituality*; Phylis Trible's *God and the Rhetoric of Sexuality*; Rosemary Radford Ruether's *New Woman New Earth, Sexist Ideologies and Human Liberation*; Mary Daly's *Beyond God the Father*; Clare Benedicks Fischer's *Women in a Strange Land*; Merlin Store's *When God Was a Woman*.[20]

Nelle Morton puts the challenge to men well. At the close of one of her papers, she addresses this paragraph "to all men who read these words":

It is well to heed the new speech of the new woman. Never have her words come from such a stance and from such assurance. They cannot be heard by listening out of "old ears". . . . But if you listen out of your wholeness (there is an organic listening as well as an organic speech), you may be able to hear what is back of her words, what is around them, and beyond them.[21]

Here are some of the thrusts in the new spiritual awareness of women that seem directly relevant to spiritual growth:

—There is an emphasis on the holistic, nondualistic, nonhierarchical, oneness of reality and a rejection of the splitting of body and spirit, secular and sacred, nature and history, rational thought and the imaginative-poetic-feeling side of persons. The divine is experienced as inherent in one's life and relationship, not "up there" or "out there."

—There is an emphasis on the organic roots of spirituality. This emphasis produces a respect for gradual growth and change and an appreciation for the natural cycles of birth and growth, of decay, death, and rebirth. Hope, in women's new spiritual experience, is rooted in their sense of participating in this process. Wholeness includes reclaiming our bodies and opening ourselves to the renewing energies of Mother Earth. This organic ecological experience becomes inseparable from the flowing experience of *transcending*, leaving behind the dualistic, static *transcendence*.[22]

—Closely related with this organic spirituality is a joyful emphasis on spontaneous dance, music, poetry, and drama as resources of enriching and celebrating the spiritual reality that infuses all of life.

—There is a healthy pluralism based on respect for the value and uniqueness of each person's spiritual journey. In this respect for differentness there is an inclusive spirit that contrasts sharply with the exclusiveness in much patriarchal Jewish, Christian, and Muslim religion.

—In the new spirituality of women, there is a keen awareness of the power of guiding images to strengthen or weaken personal identity and self-esteem. There is an emphasis, therefore, on the need of women to experience "feminine" images of spirituality to repair the damage they have suffered from experiencing the plethora of male images in both the Jewish and Christian traditions. For women there are healing, growthing energies in experiencing the nonhierarchical female images of divinity–e.g., Spirit, mother Goddess, wind, and fire (as at Pentecost).[23] As Carol P. Christ points out, women need the symbol of the Goddess to affirm the legitimacy, autonomy, and beneficence of female power.[24]

–There is an understanding of the way our dominant images limit or expand the horizons of our experiences of spiritual reality and the conviction that more inclusive spiritual images can open persons to more whole and healthy experiences of the divine in all of life. In my experience there can be healing and growth for men as well as for women in getting in touch with the energy of nonhierarchical, inclusive images from the women's spiritual heritage and allowing these to replace traditional hierarchical images of male dominance (King, Prince, Lord, Mighty One, etc.).

–There is in the new spirituality of women an explicit use of religious rituals and images to help women develop their spiritual potentials and personal strengths. Resources from women's ancient spiritual heritage are being recovered and new images and rituals created to help women rebirth themselves from inner self-oppression (resulting from internalizing the negative evaluations of their culture) and from their oppression by society's institutions.[25] Rituals that affirm the inherent spiritual worth of women can help them mobilize their strength to fight social oppression. In increasing numbers, women are getting their consciousness raised. This allows them to discover that they *are* persons with strengths and potentials, rights and responsibilities. New images and rituals are facilitating this self-other liberation process.

–There is an understanding of the way creative thoughts and actions form around one's guiding images, the way in which images tend to bring into reality what is being imaged. Thus, spiritual and political, religious and secular changes are understood as intimately interrelated. Nelle Morton states:

> I believe that the liberation of the human spirit from her captivity, the liberation of women, and the liberation of the oppressed of the earth will come at one and the same time and be

the same radical movement that will make a unity of the spiritual and the political.[26]

—There is a growing awareness among many women that women have something unique and precious to contribute to human spirituality, out of their experiences of oppression and liberation and out of their experiences as women participating in the miracle of the creation of new life within their bodies. If men are open to receive this gift, we may together evolve more enlivening images of ultimate reality.

It is clear that any understanding of spiritual reality that can energize and nourish the full becoming of women as well as that of men must be a whole theology that values women's spiritual insights and experiences as fully as it values the insights and experiences of men. What is needed (and is gradually developing) is a dynamic, growing theology that integrates and celebrates the spiritual wisdom of both women and men. Such an inclusive vision of spiritual reality will become a powerful stream of spiritual energy to nurture whole-person growth.

USING THEOLOGY IN GROWTH WORK

There are four interdependent ways in which theological reflection can be useful in facilitating growth. The first is *foundational theology*. This consists of making explicit in our minds as counselors the philosophical-theological assumptions about human beings and how they grow, which are implicit in the way we practice our art. It also involves getting in better touch with the particular spiritual heritage in which we have our roots. These awarenesses allow us to critique and change our working assumptions and to push the taproot of our counseling deeper. Making explicit our assumptions and the values derived from these assumptions, lessens the risk that we will unwittingly push our values and theological understandings onto our clients, rather than respecting their need and right to discover their own framework of meaning.

The second way of using theology to facilitate growth is *inductive theology*. If a theological idea is valid in and relevant to one's life situation, it can be experienced and tested in one's life and relationships. Living theology is not a set of abstract principles but a process of continuing discovery. Doing theology inductively consists of reflecting on meaningful experiences, in a counseling session, class, or growth group, for example, to discover what theological truths have been involved. By relating actual experiences of growth, with one's personal theology, one can allow the resources of one's heritage to undergird that growth.

In church-sponsored marriage enrichment events, I sometimes ask, after a meaningful communication exercise, "As you think about what you've experienced, what biblical images or stories come to your mind?" In the theological debriefing that follows an exercise like the box and meadow, I have seen a group of twenty-four couples quickly fill an entire chalkboard listing biblical themes that had been enlivened and illuminated for them by the experience. For many it is a new awareness to discover that biblical images can come to life in this way in a growth experience.

The third way of using theology for facilitating growth is *theological repair work*. Destructive theological beliefs, attitudes, and feelings feed many people's neurotic fears, superstitions, and guilt feelings. The "exorcism" of Henry's demon, described in the last chapter, is one technique for helping people do needed theological repair work. Clearing away such theological debris is a major and essential step in spiritual growth for many people.

A projective technique using biblical images can be used in growth groups and individual counseling to help persons from religious backgrounds identify and begin to remove spiritual growth blocks. To use this method one simply asks: "Will you tell me your favorite Bible story? Just put it in your own words." After they finish this, one can say, "Now, tell me the story you most dislike." Many biblical stories deal with archetypal themes, with feelings, conflicts, and struggles most of us experience. The selection and retelling of particular stories is like a screen on which people project their own struggles and fears, their conflicts and dilemmas. Thus they become aware of areas needing growth work.

The fourth use of theological reflection in growth work, *theological enrichment*, involves enabling people to deepen and enrich their spiritual experience intentionally. The spiritual-growth methods described in the last chapter and techniques from psychosynthesis for centering on the higher Self are useful in this type of growth work. It is often helpful to encourage people to select images they find meaningful and to meditate on these. With people who are feeling cut off from sources of nurture, it may be helpful to suggest that they meditate regularly, focusing on images such as these: "Underneath are the everlasting arms–"; "I am the bread of life–"; "As one whom his mother comforts so will I comfort you." The full therapeutic and growth-enabling uses of symbols, images, and stories from the major religious traditions of humankind have yet to be developed. The creation of such a "theotherapy" is one of the exciting challenges for the future of psychology of religion and pastoral counseling.

Time-Values Inventory

(An instrument for evaluating your life-style and using your time more intentionally and productively)

Instructions: 1. Look down the column of time-consuming activities; add activities that now use significant amounts of your time. 2. After each activity, check one of the 3 columns—*Time OK* means "The time I'm spending at present seems appropriate to me"; *More Time* means "I would like to invest more time in this"; *Less Time* means "This activity deserves less time than I'm giving it." 3. Reflect on the values inherent in your present and your desired re-allocation of time. 4. Evaluate your present and your desired uses of time in light of the criteria on p. 93 and the values you find meaningful from your own religious tradition. 5. Make any changes you now see as appropriate in the items you checked "Time OK," "More Time," and "Less Time." 6. For each activity now checked "More Time" or "Less Time," develop a plan for achieving the change you desire. Jot down the gist of your plan on the right, including *when* you will implement the plan. 7. List the benefits which will probably result from these modifications of your uses of time and the negative consequences which will result from not implementing your change plans. 8. Discuss the results of your self-inventory with your spouse or a close friend. Where appropriate, develop joint plans for changing your uses of time together. 9. Repeat this inventory periodically. 10. Each time you successfully implement a change plan, congratulate yourself for living more intentionally! Remember your time *is* your life. Use it intentionally and well.

MY TIME-CONSUMING ACTIVITIES	TIME OK	MORE TIME	LESS TIME	MY CHANGE PLANS
Work time				
Time spent sleeping				
Play time				
Time spent on my body (exercise, etc.)				
Time alone (for myself)				
Personal-spiritual growth time				
Time communicating with my spouse (or my closest friend)				
Time with my children				
Time with others I care about				
Time serving others				
Time in creative activities				
Free, unstructured time				
Time wasted				
(Other uses of my time)				

Chapter 6

Wholeness Counseling Through the Stages of Life

The willingness to move through each passage is equivalent to the willingness to live abundantly. If we don't grow, we are not really living. Growth demands a temporary surrender of security. It means giving up familiar but limiting patterns . . . The courage to take new steps allows us to let go of each stage with its satisfactions and to find the fresh responses that will release the richness of the next. The power to animate all of life's seasons is a power that resides within us.

–Gail Sheehy, *Passages: Predictable Crises of Adult Life* (New York: Dutton, 1974), pp. 353-354.

Wholeness Counseling is a developmental approach to people. When one puts on the glasses of hope and growth, each life stage, from birth to death, offers a fresh set of emerging strengths and possibilities that did not exist in previous stages. This awareness is the source of unfolding possibilities. Each stage also has within it a new set of problems, limitations, frustrations, and losses. These painful realities bring many people to counseling. The strategy of Growth Counseling is to help people deal with the problems and losses by developing the new strengths and possibilities of their particular life stage. The developmental orientation also implies a strategy of positive prevention that involves providing an abundance of easily available growth groups to help people develop the special treasures of each life stage.

The color spectrum, as in a rainbow, is an apt way of picturing the life stages. Each color, like each stage, is a valuable part of the whole, complementing the other colors. Persons in their eighties know many valuable things from their living that I cannot know. (In more age-affirming cultures, these things are recognized for what they are–wisdom.) In my present life stage I know some important things that I could not have known were it not for the ups and downs of all the previous stages. I can see and feel and do some things now that would not have been possible without these learnings. Younger people (who have grown up in a different world) know things from their experience that I cannot know, except as I am open to learning from them. Growth counseling seeks to help people discover and value the special hues of their particular life stage.

The image of the rainbow though useful does not communicate adequately the negative side of aging. Experience in the various life stages usually includes the dark hues of conflicts and crises of pain and tragedy. There are clashes among and within the dominant life experiences and values of different age groups. The rainbow must be understood in the context of violent turbulance of the storm which preceeded it.

THE DEVELOPMENT PERSPECTIVE

In the practice of counseling, therapy, and preventive growth education an understanding of lifelong growth is essential. In working with adolescents, for example, the varied problems they bring are illuminated if the counselor understands these in the context of the adolescents' central growth task–developing a sturdy sense of autonomous identity. Unfinished, confused, or diffused identity issues are at the root of many of the problems teen-agers bring to growth groups and counseling. Identity questions such as these are intertwined with the practical problem and relationship issues with which they struggle: Who am I as an individual separate from my parents? What do *I* really believe and value? What is my essential value as a unique person? What can I do with my life that will have meaning for myself and society? Finding strong, workable answers to identity questions is a continuing process throughout one's life. The answers change, in some ways, in each stage. But in adolescence, identity struggles are center stage, influencing all aspects of one's life.

As a cognitive map for facilitating growth, I use an expanded version of Erik Erikson's familiar stages of growth, corrected by insights from feminist psychologists and augmented by recent developmental studies. Wholeness is an ongoing process in which one's present growth builds, for better or worse, on all that has gone before, and is pulled forward by the promise of what can be in the future. Each developmental stage brings a new growth challenge and fresh resources. Erikson has introduced a forward thrust by his epigenetic principle which reverses the backward pull in Freud's developmental thought.[1] In commenting on this, Don Browning states:

> The meaning of life is to be found in the end of life, in the purpose of life as it expresses itself in maturity and generativity. . . . The end of life must not be understood in terms of the beginning; rather, the beginning must be understood in terms of what it contributes to and how it is directed by those emerging potentials which arise late in development but that are just as fundamental to life as that which appears earlier.[2]

There is in Erikson a sense of the flow of growth that transcends and integrates the stages. Wholeness at one stage involves all the other stages either as it builds on what occurred in earlier stages or as it prepares for what can come "in the fullness of time." The potentials of each life stage unfold according to the organism's built-in ground plan of growth, the epigenetic principle. But the process by which this occurs is never automatic, always intentional. The fulfillment of developmental possibility is the result of decision and action.[3] Effective growth work in one stage produces new strengths that are carried into the future growth stages. Unfinished growth continues to distort the process and steal the vital energies of growth in subsequent stages. There is risk at each growth stage: "Each successive step . . . is a potential crisis. . . . Crisis is used here in the developmental sense to connote not a threat of catastrophe, but a turning point, a crucial period of increased vulnerability and heightened potential."[4]

THE HISTORICAL-CULTURAL CONTEXT

Personality development is deeply interrelated with one's social milieu. According to Erikson the way a developmental stage is experienced and the resources available for growth depend, to a considerable extent, on the cultural and historical context of an individual's life. The institutions, rituals, myths, belief systems, and practices of one's culture facilitate or complicate the growthful handling of developmental crises. Contemporary Western cultures do not provide particularly nurturing environments for growth work at any stage of the life journey. For example, wholesale uprootedness and value confusion make the identity-forming task of many youths extremely difficult. In a time of gradual social change, there are resources in a culture's value consensus, its stable institutions, and in the intergenerational support structures of families that are much less available to young people today. Our culture is in a *collective identity crisis* which activates the residual anxieties about identity loss from childhood, in youth and in their parents.[5] In counseling with troubled youth and their parents it sometimes helps to share one's awareness of this fact by saying to them, "It's not an easy time to be a teen-ager, or the parents of a teen-ager."

The male biases of our culture have tended to distort our understanding of human development. The disciplines of psychotherapy and psychology have been dominated by the male perspective and experience. Without our being aware of it, thought about growth has been largely in terms of the mental image of a male.

This fact has constricted our understanding of growth for both women and men. The vast majority of the differences in the ways males and females develop psychologically probably are the result of the diverse ways boys and girls are socialized in their particular cultures. How many developmental differences are biologically based cannot be determined until that time when both sexes are allowed free opportunity to develop their full potential. It seems likely that most of the differences are sociocultural and not biological. What is certain now is that the constrictions all cultures place on growth for both girls and boys encourage the development of lopsided rather than whole persons.

The model of growth by which boys and men have been socialized in traditional Western cultures emphasizes moving away from the attributes identified with women–dependency, passivity, feelingfulness, caretaking, and emotional closeness to others–and toward the so-called "masculine" qualities of rationality, aggressiveness, competitiveness, achievement, and conquest. The traditional cultural growth model for girls and women emphasizes the opposite of these characteristics. Women are programmed not to grow toward the "unfeminine" attributes. They are encouraged to derive their identity from the man they marry and from their role as a child-rearer. Thus, they are discouraged from finding their autonomous identity as persons and discouraged from developing capacities that are useful outside the context of the family such as assertiveness and achievement.

Erikson has been criticized appropriately by feminist thinkers for his views concerning the way growth is defined in women: Mature fulfillment for women centers on the fact that their bodies have an " 'inner space' destined to bear the offspring of chosen men, and with it, a biological, psychological and ethical commitment to take care of human infancy."[6] In effect, a woman doesn't have a full identity until she knows whom she will marry and for whom she will make a home. Erikson failed to see that what he was describing is the way women *are* in a sexist society, not the way they must or could be in a more growthful culture.

THE DEVELOPMENTAL ROLE OF RELIGION

Our ability to develop a self and to feel its reality depends without question on our psychological development. But what religious traditions tell us is that psychological development is not enough to give us a sense of being real and fully in touch with life. Religion tells us bluntly that a "good life" is a life lived consciously in relation to God, to mystery as it comes into our own lives.[7]

In this statement Ann Ulanov points to the crucial importance of the spiritual dimension in human development. From a growth perspective, the function of one's spiritual life and one's community of faith is to undergird and nurture one's total growth through the life cycle. Erikson's brilliant psychohistorical studies of Luther and Gandhi illuminate the interrelations of religious growth and total personal growth, in a particular historical-cultural context.[8] The research of Lawrence Kohlberg on the developmental stages of morality and conscience complements the work of Erikson.[9] Carol Gilligan's *In a Different Voice: Psychological Theory and Women's Development* (Cambridge: Harvard University Press, 1983) challenges Kohlberg's stages and describes significant differences in women's moral and psychological development. Studies by LeRoy Aden, John J. Gleason, Jr., and James W. Fowler III have explored the developmental understanding of faith in some depth.[10] Insights from these studies offer practical resources for facilitating spiritual growth.

A salugenic faith is an evolving, growing faith. As Aden states, "Faith . . . participates in the life cycle of the individual who possesses it . . . the dominant form that faith takes at any one time is determined in part by the particular development stage in which the individual is immersed."[11] A static belief system blocks the flowering of living salugenic spirituality. Wholeness-nurturing faith at a particular life stage is faith that enables and energizes the fulfillment of the central growth task of that stage.

To highlight the usefulness of the development perspective in growth work, here is an overview of the life stages with particular reference to spiritual growth. I have modified Erikson's eight stages by dividing stages 5 through 8. I have done this to emphasize the dramatic differences of these sub-stages for people who have children.

It is clear that growth issues for single and childless persons, at the various life stages, are experienced very differently. In our family-centered society, the stages of creative singlehood, or creative marriage without children, have been given very little attention by developmental psychologists. At least until recently, single people have been made to feel inferior or even deviant. Unmarried women have had a special burden. As Jean Baker Miller says, "No matter what their other accomplishments, most carried within them a sense that they were second-class people, unworthy and unwanted."[12] Fortunately, this has begun to change. There is an increasing respect for other life-styles and types of relationships, in addition to the traditional marriage and family patterns. More options, including the choices not to marry and not to have children, are opening up to people in our society.

Stage 1: INFANCY (birth to 15 months). The key growth need of an infant during this period is to develop a deep conviction that existence is trustworthy. Parents themselves must feel enough trust (in themselves, each other, life, and God) so that the small children can "catch" a sense of basic trust from them empathetically. There must be sufficient nurture and trust in the parents' own lives to enable them to respond warmly and dependably to the physical and emotional needs of the child. If "basic trust" comes to outweigh mistrust in the infant, the strength that emerges is *hope*. Erikson declares: "Hope is both the earliest and the most indispensable virtue inherent in the state of being alive. Hope is the ontogenetic basis of faith, and is nourished by the adult faith which pervades patterns of care."[13]

Basic trust and hope are the foundation of all subsequent personality development. They are also the root of salugenic religion. How can the positive contagion of trust and hope be nurtured in close relationships in an era with a trust-hope vacuum like ours? Erikson holds that the parental faith that undergirds trust and hope in the newborn has sought its safeguards institutionally (and found its greatest enemy, on occasion) in organized religions. He emphasizes the way in which religion functions to renew parental trust:

It is religion which by way of ritual methods offers man [sic] a periodic collective restitution of basic trust which in adults ripens to a continuation of faith and realism. . . . The query of the psychologist and that of the theologian meet in the consideration of one common question . . . whether or not a given form of organized religion at a given time and in a given community is or is not able to accomplish that systematic reassurance of the adults which is necessary for reliable transmission of basic reassurance to small children. . . . I know only too well that whenever organized religion fails there remains in human life a very basic void which is not taken care of by the mere denial of faith or by an irrational overevaluation of substitute dogmas. He who believes that he can do without religion obligates himself to a new accounting for very basic human needs.[14]

This statement has profound implications for the programs of churches and synagogues! These institutions have only scratched the surface of what they could do to nurture trust in parents. Participating in a small trust-renewing mutual-care group can be invaluable for effective parenting. Couples classes, parent-training courses, preparation for parenting workshops, single-parents support groups, and marriage-enrichment events can provide parents with trust- and hope-feeding experiences within a growth group. Parents of young children have the future at their fingertips, literally. Helping them become more life-affirming within themselves and their intimate relationships empowers their ability to transmit trust to the next generation.

It is vitally important that fathers as well as mothers become deeply involved in the intimate care of children from infancy through adolescence. In most cultures, at present, almost all the initial personality-forming experiences of boys and girls are in relationship to a woman, usually a mother. Mother-monopolized child rearing, as developed in patriarchal cultures, has deleterious effects on the parents, on the children, and on the wider society. When the intimate need-satisfaction of small children is socially defined as the almost exclusive responsibility of mothers, many women feel burdened and trapped by this heavy load of physical and emotional dependency. In this situation, men are deprived of the satisfactions and growth potentials that are present for both men and women in fairly shared parenting. When mothering is socially defined as the essential and primary source of self-worth for women, the full potentializing of many mothers is thereby restricted. Non-mothers are deprived of basic identity and esteem. As a highly significant study by Adrienne Rich declares, mothering so narrowly defined has "ghettoized and degraded female potentialities."[15]

There is increasing evidence that mother-dominated child rearing causes and/or contributes to many prevalent personality problems that diminish growth for persons throughout their lives.[16] "Normal" personality with its plethora of problems, in most cultures, is mother-reared personality. Many males grow up haunted by powerful anxiety feelings from their overly intense early experiences with mother and their lack of balancing experiences with father. These subconscious, conflicted feelings often include fears of the magical, life-and-death power ascribed to women with the accompanying feeling that one can survive only by dependence on a woman. A deep fear of dependence on women, rooted in fears of the magical power attributed to them in childhood, causes many men to fight and deny their need for healthy interdependence in a variety of self-other hurting, "macho" ways. Having never learned to practice or value mutual nurturing, the rich potential of men to enjoy receiving and giving nurture is largely undeveloped. They are alienated from their soft, vulnerable feelings and from close mutually nurturing relationships. Consequently, they must meet their legitimate dependency needs in hidden, manipulative, and guilt-ridden ways.

Women, in contrast, are programmed in patriarchal cultures to define and value themselves mainly as nurturers of others, to get their own nurture by seeming weak and childishly dependent on men, and to not develop many of their potential strengths. A woman who feels weak, undernurtured, and chronically overloaded by full-time parenting cannot possibly satisfy adequately the demanding emotional needs of small children, nor can she really enjoy and grow from the creative dimensions of parenting.

Parents of young children should be challenged to see that nothing is more vital for the future than "people-making" (Virginia Satir's term), the development of wholeness in the next generation. They should be encouraged to understand that this process is much too important for either men or women to be excluded from deep involvement in it. They should be helped to devise fair, feasible ways (which is often difficult in our society) to share both intimate parenting and, if they choose, work outside the home.

Stage 2: EARLY CHILDHOOD (15 months to 3 years). A child's basic growth task in this stage is to develop a robust sense of *autonomy* based on a foundation of trust learned in the first stage. The danger is that shame and doubt will overpower autonomy. The new strength that is derived from growing autonomy is *will*. In counseling and growth groups, parents of a child in this age group need to be encouraged to support the child's need to become an autonomous self (who can say no and mean it), without losing the secure sense of trustful dependency. To be able to do this, parents must develop their own sense of self, their own autonomy. Women whose primary identity is derived from the identity of their husbands cannot prize and support fully the needs of their children for growing autonomy.

Stage 3: PRESCHOOL AGE (3 to 6 years). The central growth tasks of children in this stage are to develop *initiative* and to learn to relate warmly and securely with the parent of the other sex. The new strength that develops is *purpose.* The growth danger is that a sense of guilt will outweigh feelings of initiative. Parents need to be encouraged to give children space to exercise and strengthen the thrust of their personalities. Many parents also may need help in accepting a child's need for a close relationship with the parent (or other adult) of the other sex. A child who develops warm, good feelings in this relationship has a strong foundation for all future relationships with persons of the other sex. Marriage enrichment that deepens the bond between parents can be of great value in this stage. It can help them accept their children's need for closeness with the other-sexed parent without feeling that their relationship is threatening. Solo parents in this and other stages need close nurturing relationships with other adults so that they will not exploit their children emotionally in an attempt to satisfy their own needs.

Only to the extent that parents have come to accept their own autonomy and value their assertive initiative will they be able to support their children's expressions of autonomy and initiative. The religion of parents, if it is moralistic or authoritarian, can reinforce the negative side of children's growth conflicts in stages 2 and 3 by increasing their sense of shame, self-doubt, and guilt. In contrast, salugenic religion can strengthen the parents' self-acceptance by the awareness that God affirms our unique personhood including the autonomous assertiveness of our lives.

The differences in the kinds of growth that are rewarded in boys and girls in the first three stages of development (and beyond) must now be highlighted. Even if they grow up in the same family, a little girl and a little boy grow up in different worlds because of the contrasting ways they are treated. *Autonomy* and *initiative,* the growth tasks of boys in stages 2 and 3, are not valued to the same degree or in the same way in girls. Girls in traditional families tend to be taught to develop our culture's "feminine" attributes–to be compliant, sweet, pretty, caretaking, and noncompetitive. Boys tend to be taught to value their strength and assertiveness. Psychiatrist Jean Baker Miller has observed that new models of what constitutes growth are desperately needed for both girls and boys:

> Clearly a new model for childhood is required. . . . Members of one sex need not be raised to believe that their ultimate goal is to assume a role in which they will be permitted to serve others [men]. Members of the other sex need not be raised to believe that they are superior and are to be serviced by lesser human beings while they struggle to succeed in doing the important work of the world.[17]

Stage 4: GRAMMAR-SCHOOL AGE (6 to adolescence). The growth tasks of this stage are *industry* and firming up one's sexual identity by close relations with the same-sexed parent (or a parent substitute) and same-sexed age peers. Industry involves learning the skills and tools that are valued in one's culture. The strength that accrues from this growth is a sense of *competence*. The danger is that a sense of inferiority will become stronger than the sense of competence. Parent support groups can help parents respond constructively to the growth hazards that many children encounter in our schools. Recognizing children's successes, large or small, in mastering academic and social skills reinforces their emerging sense of competence and helps them overcome feelings of inferiority. I have described elsewhere a variety of ways in which growth groups can be used with both children and their parents at this and other stages.[18]

It is vitally important during this stage that children be able, by observing their parents and others, to form liberating images of what it is to be a whole person relating to another whole person. Some fathers communicate a truncated image of masculinity to their sons *and* daughters. And some mothers offer impoverished images of femininity to their daughters and sons. Nonsexist child-raising involves encouraging both boys and girls to develop their full range of competence and interests, including those that do not fit a culture's sexist definitions of the roles appropriate to each sex.[19]

The values reflected in parents' life-style can help children learn the tools of their culture growthfully. The Protestant Ethic, which equates goodness with hard work and success, alienates many adults from enlivening spontaneity and play. A new wholeness ethic that emphasizes using one's gifts well in work *and* play can undergird growth in the fourth stage. By seeking to live such an ethic in their life-style, parents can help children learn to value, intermingle, and balance work and play.

Stage 5: EARLY ADOLESCENCE (the onset of puberty to 15 or 16). The growth task of stages 5 and 6 is firming up of one's *identity* as an autonomous person of one sex. The growth danger in adolescence is identity diffusion, the lack of a clear sense of who one is as a separate person. The new strength that results from the growth is *fidelity.* Maturing sexuality makes it essential for adolescents to learn constructive ways of relating to the other sex. A variety of models of identity-strengthening and relationship-skills groups are available to help youth with these central growth tasks.[20] Many parents need growth-support groups during these years to cope constructively with a double load–their own mid-years crises and the stresses of being parents of adolescents. Such parents often need encouragement in gradually relaxing their control so that their daughters and sons will have space to grow without severe self-other hurting rebellion. Transgenerational communication workshops can help bridge the youth-parents gap which sometimes widens to a yawning chasm.

Stage 6: LATER ADOLESCENCE (16 to 21). Identity-formation work continues and focuses increasingly on preparation for young adulthood during this stage. For many young persons these years involve such crucial decisions as leaving their childhood home, making vocational commitments, and choosing a mate. Growth groups focusing on vocational choices and on long-range preparation for marriage or for creative singlehood can be valuable during this stage.

Identity formation in stages 5 and 6 can be strengthened by the spiritual searching and discoveries of youth. Salugenic faith undergirds the identity-strengthening awareness that "It's good to be me!" Growth-enabling religion encourages youth and young adults to search for their own meanings and develop their own functional beliefs and values, distilled from but often transcending their family's religious and value tradition. Healthy religion can help inspire adolescents to find their "cause," to commit themselves to something bigger than themselves that is challenging and worthwhile for humankind.

Many students of human development have assumed that adolescence is a time of expansion and growing autonomy for girls as it is for boys. Clara Thompson first observed that for many girls it is exactly the reverse–a period when growth options become constricted. Psychologists Judith M. Bordwick and Elizabeth Douvan describe this growth-limiting process as it is experienced by many girls:

> Until adolescence the idea of equal capacity, opportunity, and life style is held out to them. But sometime in adolescence the message becomes clear that one had better not do too well, that competition is aggressive and unfeminine . . . the girl responds to the single clear directive–she withdraws from what is clearly masculine. In high school and increasingly in college, girls . . . perceive the establishment of interpersonal goals [getting married and having children] as the most salient route to identity. This results in the maximization of interpersonal skills, an interpersonal view of the world, a withdrawal from the development of independence, activity, ability and competition.

Thus, many adolescent and young adult women are not encouraged to develop a strong sense of authentic, independent identity in relation to other people and the world. Instead they are encouraged to flee into marriage.

> When one is anxious or uncertain about one's femininity, a viable technique for quelling those anxious feelings is an exaggerated conformity, a larger-than-life commitment to *Kinder, Küche, Kirche.* . . . And she can be more certain that the feedback will assure her of her femininity.[21]

A study of the self-esteem scores of high school and college students showed that the self-esteem of males was significantly higher than that of females. Androgynous persons (scoring high in both attributes that our culture defines as "feminine" and those defined as "masculine") had the highest self-esteem scores, but these didn't differ significantly from those of the "masculine-typed" person. Consistent with other such studies, the findings indicated "that successful socialization into the feminine role is accompanied by low levels of self-regard."[22]

Stage 7: EARLY YOUNG ADULTHOOD (premarriage and early marriage before children arrive). Compared to the stages through adolescence, relatively little attention has been given to the adult growth stages. Erikson's discussion of the postadolescent growth crises is relatively sweeping, thematic, and brief. From the empirical studies that have been done, it is evident that the adult stages are times of significant and continuing changes in one's self-definition, in career meanings, in sense of time, and in all one's significant relationships–with spouse, children, and parents.

The relatively static, hope-diminishing view of adulthood that has dominated the self-definition of most adults simply does not fit the fact that dynamic changes occur throughout adult life.[23] The growth task of the young adult stages is to establish the capacity for *intimacy* from which emerges a new strength–self-giving *love.* If the capacity for intimacy does not flourish, one may develop a sense of painful isolation. Giving oneself to another with intimate abandon and joy is possible only when one has a firm sense of personal identity. Growth issues that are encountered frequently in counseling with young adults include unfinished identity struggles, severing ties of emotional dependency on parents, learning competence in a vocation that will let them use their maximum potentials, developing the skills of mutually satisfying intimacy with a person of the other sex, and struggling to integrate sex within relationships of mutual respect, equality, and love.

Religion facilitates intimacy when it enables people to discover how to integrate intellectual, emotional, sexual, and spiritual sharing. Youth and young adults (as well as older adults) need a "sensual spirituality" (Matthew Fox's phrase) that allows them to say yes to their bodies and to integrate their sexual passions with caring, respect, and mutual responsibility. They need to discover that mutual pleasuring can be more ecstatic when it is in a relationship where "soul touches soul," as a member of a young adult growth group put it.

Many young people flee into marriage to escape their own feelings of loneliness, inadequacy, identity diffusion, and unhappiness in their families. Young adult growth groups should help people become free to *choose* singlehood or marriage. Such groups should focus on self-growth and on strengthening relationship-building skills. Learning how to have both a satisfying inner life and a fulfilling relational life is the best preparation for either creative marriage or creative singlehood.

Some churches are experimenting with innovative models of premarriage preparation that do not depend mainly on a few rushed sessions before the wedding. They are encouraging couples to participate in a small pre-wedding enrichment class, group, or retreat. In these groups, couples learn love-nurturing communication and conflict resolution skills. Whatever form pre-wedding preparation takes, it should be seen as the beginning of an ongoing process of intentional enrichment after the wedding.[24]

Over the last two decades I have had the good fortune of working intensively with a considerable number of young adults, both singles and couples, in a theological seminary setting. This is a challenging age group with whom to work. Many of these persons are refreshingly open and interested in both personal and relationship growth work.

Stage 8: MIDDLE YOUNG ADULTHOOD (with children in the preschool years). A new generation is begun in the family life cycle in this exciting, demanding stage! The needs of parents, mentioned in discussing childhood stages 1, 2, and 3 come into sharp focus. A warm growing style of living and sharing is the best gift parents can give children in these stages. But, this is very difficult for many young adults because they are in a period of pressure-cooker stresses. Their family system has been altered drastically, sometimes traumatically, by the entry of a new baby into their marital relationship. Often they struggle with the multiple pressures of finishing school, moving to a new community, learning vocational and marital skills at the same time that they must learn the demanding skills of parenting. Unfinished growth work frequently is stirred up, on a subconscious level, in parents and in their marriage, by interaction with their child in particular stages.

It is imperative that parents of preschool children have much more support, encouragement, and training in parenting skills and nurture of their own growth than most now receive. Marriage enrichment for couples is crucial since the possibilities for either marital growth or marital disintegration are heightened by the heavy life pressures of this stage. Enriching the marital bond may be what is needed most to enhance parent-child relationships.

Festivals of growth are one of the ways in which families can celebrate the significant growth events in their lives together. Some of these can be linked with established church rituals such as infant dedication or baptism. But, in addition, the satisfactions of family life can be deepened by other mini-celebrations of significant growth steps by family members–e.g., becoming pregnant, the birth of a baby, a child's first words, the couple's success in revising their marriage covenant periodically to make it fairer and more just, etc. Such celebrations are ways of lifting and affirming those precious moments when the miracle of continuing growth is most evident.

Stage 9: LATER YOUNG ADULTHOOD (children in grammar school). As in stage 8 many parents carry a double load at this stage–heavy child-centered responsibilities and the demands on both parents of having jobs outside the home. What often is neglected in this crunch is the parents' self-nurture and the nurture of their relationship. If such self-neglect continues for long, it eventually impoverishes the marriage and this diminishes parental effectiveness. It is important for churches and the continuing education programs of schools to provide abundant opportunities for single parents and couples to develop their own creative talents and interests as well as receive parent skills training.

Stage 10: EARLY MID-YEARS (adolescent children in stages 5 and 6). The growth task of the mid-years is generativity. The danger in this stage is that sense of self-absorption will outweigh *generativity*. The new strength that emerges when generativity flourishes is *care*. *Generativity* can be defined as self-fulfillment through self-investment in the ongoing human enterprise. "In this stage, a man and a woman must have defined for themselves what and whom they have come to care for, what they care to do well, and how they plan to take care of what they have started and created."[25] Generativity involves caring about and for the future by investing something of yourself in those persons, values, and causes that may live after you and that may help to make our planet a more wholeness-nurturing place for the whole human family.

This stage for many people is a time when they are savoring life and contributing in satisfying and sometimes exhausting ways to their families, their jobs, their churches, and their communities. Some couples find the mid-years a fulfilling time of rejuvenated intimacy and aliveness in their individual lives. But many people do not discover or develop the new possibilities of the mid-years. Such persons are resigned to "things as they are"–flat, boring, and without challenge. Quiet and painful mid-years crises often bring people to counseling, therapy, and growth groups. Many mid-years persons attempt to escape boredom and fear of aging by compulsive work, sexual affairs, excessive drugs, and alcohol. These escapes often compound the sense of emptiness, despair, and the fear of aging and death.

The mid-years confront many of us with a spiritual and values crisis. Increasingly, life is restructured in terms of time-left-to-live rather than time-since-birth. The painful awareness that one's time is limited causes some people to question the basic meaning of their life-style.[26] Many mid-years people feel caught between aging parents with declining health and needy adolescents. These pressures motivate some persons to reformulate their values and to engage more intentionally in personal growth and spiritual renewal activities.

At no time of life is the growth-hope perspective on one's life more valuable than during the mid-years. Our youth-idolizing culture has brainwashed us to believe that "the action" is mainly for the young and that exciting growth probably isn't possible after the young-adult years. Our society's flat, static view of adulthood is the result, in part, of Freud's fallacious belief that our personalities are relatively fixed after adolescence. It isn't surprising that studies have shown an increase in feelings of inferiority after the mid-forties.[27] I suspect that most people in this age group could chuckle with some comfort at a cartoon I saw recently. It depicted a psychologist saying to a mid-years man: "You did very well on your IQ test! You're a man of forty-nine with the intelligence of fifty-three."

Numerous studies of the adult life stages have demonstrated the inaccuracy of this fatalistic static view of adulthood. They have confirmed what many of us had already learned from experience, that the mid-years *can* be a satisfying, growthful "prime of life." These years were for me the most fulfilling period of my life up to then. They were also a turbulent time of accelerating painful losses.

The mid-years and beyond are a recent gift to humankind. The dramatic increase in the life expectancy in this century has created several new, potentially creative life stages for the majority of people in developed countries. Many of us are living long enough and are healthy enough to enjoy an active life through the fifth, sixth, and even the seventh and eighth decades. What we need are new strategies to help us use these new years well and enjoy them fully. Elsewhere I have described such strategies utilizing mid-years generativity groups and growth methods.[28]

Stage 11: LATER MID-YEARS (the empty nest, preretirement period). This stage is very different from the early mid-years. The gradually emptying nest confronts couples who have had child-centered families with the pressing need to revitalize their marriage. The mid-years crisis is particularly painful for many women. The menopause, empty nest, and declining physical attractiveness (as measured by the culture's superficial criteria of youthfulness) constitute a triple blow to the self-esteem of women who have gained a sense of identity and worth mainly from being attractive, "successful" mothers and wives. Jean Baker Miller states:

> Women who may have avoided the task of building a valid sense of identity in adolescence and early adulthood now face even worse anguish at a time when they have much less chance of finding a solution. Society's devaluation of anyone past youth adds its fearful effect. This disparagement falls particularly heavily on women since they have been valued primarily for their physical attributes.[29]

Menopausal depression results, to a considerable extent, from the constructing effects of our sexist culture on the growth of strong identity and self-esteem in women.

Many mid-years women need encouragement and help in discovering how they can best develop their latent abilities and use their time and energy in fulfilling ways as the nest empties. Fortunately an increasing number of mid-years women are finding new zest in developing the potentials that were unused in earlier phases of their life. Many young adult women are reducing the probability that the mid-years will be so traumatic by developing more autonomy and more of their potentials long before the nest begins to empty.

Taking part in an effective feminist consciousness-raising group can be a strengthening, esteem-enhancing experience for a woman at any stage. This can be particularly growthful for mid-years women. In such support groups, they will be helped to understand their own aging in ways that foster feelings of self-acceptance and self-worth. They may become aware of the ancient heritage of women's wisdom in which older women were respected for their valuable wisdom and the insights gained from their life experiences as women.[30] In a consciousness-raising group, they will be encouraged to reject the culture's negative evaluation of older women and to develop the positive potential of their mature years.

A vivid illustration of the power of self-fulfilling beliefs about aging is in the area of mid-years sexuality. The widely believed fallacy that people decline sharply in their sexual powers and pleasure capacities after forty-five or fifty is one of the reasons many people do decline. Studies of human sexuality show convincingly that "if you use it, you usually won't lose it." If you believe that you can go on enjoying the good gift of your sexuality, you probably will, into the seventh and eighth decades (barring some unusual physical problem) with gradual decrease in frequency but no decrease in pleasure.[31]

Because the mid-years are a new stage of life, there is a poverty of meaningful rituals for celebrating significant growth events during these years. A "generativity festival" in a congregation is one way of celebrating the ways in which people are investing themselves in their community. Such a festival helps recognize and encourage life-styles of outreach to the needs of others in the community. One church on the West Coast recently developed a marriage-enrichment group for empty-nest couples. Participants found that within such a group, mid-years growth can be both enhanced and celebrated.

Grief growth groups are an excellent way of helping mid-years people handle constructively the accelerating losses of these and subsequent years. Learning to cope with losses without being devastated by them is an essential skill for continuing growth in the mid-years and beyond. Unfaced and unfinished "grief work" is a major cause of blocked growth in people all through the life cycle. In my experience, repressed, unfinished grief for my sister (who died when I was four) caused me to waste life energy well into my mid-years. When I finally opened this still-festering wound and let it heal, the increase of energy was striking. No type of group in the life of a church can contribute more to the healing and growth of persons throughout the latter adult years than a grief growth group.[32]

Stage 12: RETIREMENT YEARS. These are years when intentionality and the growth perspective are essential resources for using fully the new opportunities created by retirement. Many people must deal with grief feelings from the loss of job satisfactions, learn to relate to their spouses more hours in the week, and discover ways of using their newly available time for creative activities and satisfying volunteer work that sustain zest and purpose in living. For couples whose relationship has, like good wine, mellowed and improved with age, these years can include rich sharing. As the couple in Eugene O'Neill's play *Ah, Wilderness* declares: "Spring isn't everything. There's a lot to be said for fall and winter, too, if you're together."[33] But beyond sharing, it is crucial that both individuals continue to develop their own inner resources and autonomy so as to avoid the overdependency that will cripple one of them when the other partner dies.

The growth task of the retirement years is what Erikson calls *ego integrity*, the opposite of which is despair. Ego integrity means accepting one's finitude, making peace with the passing years and with the inevitable frustration of some of one's dreams. It means affirming the fragments of meaning and joy and wisdom one has found. It means living and enjoying as much as possible the precious here-and-now moment. This acceptance of life as basically good, in spite of its tragedies and losses, frees one to keep on living and growing until one dies rather than cutting off one's aliveness in remorse, meaninglessness, and despair. The strength that results from ego integrity is *wisdom*. Ego integrity is the cumulative result of growth throughout the life cycle. One's personal faith and philosophy of life can be valuable resources in undergirding ego integrity.

Stage 13: WIDOWHOOD OR WIDOWERHOOD. As suggested above, to make these years good requires intentionally developing one's inner resources in the previous stages. It also requires doing one's grief work after the spouse's death so that the wound can heal and some of the energy from that important relationship can be reinvested in living and in relating to other persons. As the widows-to-widows program has demonstrated, persons who have been through grief experiences often are the best equipped to help others cope with similar loss. Such self-other help programs show that the healing of our own loss wounds often is facilitated by reaching out to help others. With the average life expectancy of women in North America, now exceeding that of men by nearly nine years it is essential that churches and other institutions develop effective programs for enabling women (both before and after the loss of their husband) to live as full persons with their own identity and resources rather than as psychological appendages of their husband.

Stage 14: APPROACHING DEATH. As Elisabeth Kübler-Ross has shown, the process of dying for some people can be "the final stage of growth." A study by Raymond G. Carey of terminally ill patients showed that the *quality* of their religious orientation was highly correlated with their emotional adjustment to dying.[34] Those who had integrated their beliefs into their life-style tended to have the most constructive responses to dying. Having been close to another person who accepted dying with inner peace was also found to be correlated with one's own response to a terminal illness. Apparently, ego integrity and serenity in facing death are "caught," empathetically to some degree, from meaningful persons in our lives.

Here is Erikson's summary of the new interdependent strengths, or "virtues," as he calls them, that result from growth during each life stage:

> I will . . . speak of *Hope, Will, Purpose,* and *Competence* as the rudiments of virtue developed in childhood; of *Fidelity* as the adolescent virtue; and *Love, Care,* and *Wisdom* as the central virtues of adulthood. In all their seeming discontinuity, these qualities depend on each other. Will cannot be trained until hope is secure, nor can love become reciprocal until fidelity has proved reliable. Also each virtue . . . is vitally interrelated to other segments of human development, such as the stages of psychosexuality . . . , the psychosocial crises, and the steps of cognitive maturation.[35]

These strengths are transmitted from generation to generation. The development of *fidelity* in adolescents is reinforced by experiencing the strength of *care* in their mid-years parents, which in turn is reinforced by their experiencing *ego integrity* in their aging parents. Thus, the strengths and limitations of each generation are transmitted as a transgenerational spiritual heritage. Children who have a close, warm relationship with grandparents who respond to aging with serenity rooted in ego integrity, receive a precious legacy from those grandparents. This legacy can help them experience life as a journey of continuing growth, with ups and downs, with new pain and problems, but with new vistas and possibilities at each major turn in the road.

EXPERIENCING THE GROWTH PROBLEMS AND POTENTIALS OF YOUR LIFE STAGE

The purpose of this exercise is to encourage your exploration and use of the unique growth possibilities of the present.

Close your eyes and get in touch with your feelings, negative and positive, about your current life stage. / Now, on the left side of a sheet of paper, list the major problems and frustrations, pressures and losses of your present life stage. / Close your eyes and become aware of how you feel now. / In a column down the middle of the page, list all the assets and strengths, positive challenges, and new possibilities life holds for you at present. / Become aware of how you feel now. / Reflect on how you can use the assets and potentialities in the middle column to handle the problems on the left more creatively. / In the space on the right, jot down ideas about what you want to do to develop more of the possibilities of your present life stage. / Discuss your experience thoroughly with your spouse or, if you're single, with a close friend. This exercise can be used productively in individual and couple counseling and in growth groups with persons at any life stage.

Chapter 7

Summary and Conclusion

Developing Your Own Wholeness-Centered Approaches to Counseling and Therapy, Education, and Life Enhancement

As a summary of the Growth Counseling model, let me now compare the main thrusts of this approach with those of traditional psychoanalytically and insight-oriented psychotherapies. I will state the characteristics of each orientation in their extreme forms to make the contrasts clearer than they are in actual practice. It is important to emphasize the fact that many traditional therapies include significant growth emphases and insights. There are, of course, many variations in both theory and practice among traditional therapies that are not recognized in the generalizations about these approaches in the column on the left.

Traditional Therapies	**Growth Counseling/Therapy**
Based on the pathology model.	Based on the growth model.
The primary goal is to repair personality pathology to enable the person to cope effectively with life.	The primary goal is facilitating the maximum development of potentials through the life cycle.
Focus mainly on problems, weaknesses, failures, conflicts, and pathology, especially as these are related to unconscious processes and repression.	Focuses primary attention on strengths, assets, and potentialities; and views failures, trappedness, "sickness" in the wider context of wholeness.

Define *health* as the *absence* of gross pathology or maladaptive behavior, and the ability of the ego to cope with inner and outer reality.

Defines *health* as the increasing use of one's potentialities, the *presence* of a high degree of unfolding wholeness (in addition to the absence of major pathology).

View personal and relationship problems as caused by such factors as childhood trauma, neurotic processes, and blocked psychosexual development.

Views personal and relationship problems as symptoms of unlived life, diminished use of one's potentialities, blocked growth, and faulty learning. Pathological symptoms diminish as people grow.

Understand people as pushed to change by the pain of the "pathology" of fixated development in the past.

Understands people as also pulled to change by their need to grow and their hope for a more fulfilled life in the future.

View people as determined, to a greater or lesser degree, by their past experiences and relationships.

Views people as capable, to an appreciable degree, of intentionally changing obsolete or destructive feelings and behavior from the past, and of developing a more constructive life in the present and future.

Focus change efforts primarily within the psyche of individuals or, at the most, within their relationships.

Focuses change efforts in all 7 of the interdependent dimensions of a person's life and relationships and on the wider social systems that diminish or enable growth in one's community and culture.

Focus primary therapeutic attention on the unconscious aspects of the psyche.

Focuses on all levels of the psyche, conscious and unconscious.

Aim primarily at achieving insight and thus changing destructive attitudes, feelings, and self-concepts with the assumption that behavioral change will follow.

Aims at direct change of growth-diminishing attitudes, feelings, and self-concepts on the one hand, and growth-diminishing behavior patterns on the other.

Tend to see new developmental stages primarily in terms of new problems to be solved, complicated by unresolved problems from the past.

Also sees each development stage as a new set of problems *and* possibilities for growth.

See crises mainly as traumas, problems, or stress periods (which revive old unresolved problems) with which persons must cope.

Also sees crises as challenges that confront us with both the need and the opportunity to develop new strengths and learn new skills for living constructively.

Have tended to remain strongly male-oriented and to define growth in "male" ways that restrict wholeness for both women and men.

Seeks to utilize insights from male but also from the feminist psychologists and therapists to facilitate androgynous wholeness in women and men.

Have tended to see spiritual and ethical growth as either irrelevant to or as derived from emotional and interpersonal growth.

Sees spiritual and ethical growth as central, enabling dynamics in all areas of a person's growth.

The process usually involves longer-term depth analysis of the psychological factors from the past seen as causing the fixation of development and the present problems.

The process of therapy involves working in many dimensions of a person's life, using a variety of action-oriented, shorter-term, integrative methods focusing on the present and future as well as on the past.

The counselor-therapist tends to be seen as an "expert" authority-figure on the hierarchical doctor-patient model.	The counselor-therapist is seen as a skilled guide and coach for one's growth journey, a person who also needs to continue growing. Mutual growth work among peers is encouraged.
Focus mainly on helping those who have major problems in living and relating.	Focuses on facilitating growth in both those whose development is severely diminished and in those who wish to increase their already appreciable effectiveness in living.

DEVELOPING YOUR OWN UNIQUE GROWTH APPROACHES

In its basic philosophy, Wholeness Counseling is an open, evolving approach to facilitating growth through counseling and therapy, education, and life enhancement. The growth orientation calls us to stay open to our own experiences and to the future. It challenges us to stay responsive to the pull of our own future toward new, unexpected developments that will make many of our present understandings and "certainties" obsolete. When the growth perspective and principles (summarized on the right above) are the guiding orientation in the personal and professional lives of counselors, therapists, and teachers new insights and methods for growth tend to emerge in their thinking and practice.

I encourage you to use the principles and methods you've encountered in this book as resources for developing your own creative modalities using the growth-enabling theme. The approaches you develop should utilize your strengths, insights, and awareness as a unique person. I trust that you will select, adapt, and modify what I have presented, adding insights and methods from many sources including your own life experiences. As I mentioned at the beginning of this book, Wholeness Counseling aims at providing a unifying conceptual framework within which the therapeutic-growth resources from a variety of therapies and from the Hebrew and Christian traditions can be integrated in a coherent way. In developing and enriching your own approach, let me urge you to draw on the wealth of growth resources available in contemporary psychotherapies. In a companion volume, *Contemporary Growth Therapies: Resources for Actualizing Human Wholeness*, I will describe other insights and techniques that have proved useful to me in facilitating growth.

When one views counseling, education, and therapy from an open, growth perspective, it becomes clear that taking any theory uncritically or too seriously is counterproductive of growth in any such relationship. Such attitudes diminish the counselor-therapist-teacher's own creative contribution to the process of responding to the special growth needs of a particular person. This principle applies, of course, to Wholeness Counseling as fully as to any other approach. So although I hope your enthusiasm has been aroused by the main thrust of this book, I encourage you to stay in a critical, experimental, flowing, and playful space as you use these ideas to develop your own growth approach. You'll be a more effective growth enabler if you are able to chuckle at the human tendency (mine and yours) to absolutize and idolize those fragments of truth that have become illuminated in our own experience.

YOUR PERSONAL-PROFESSIONAL GROWTH

The creative changes that I have witnessed in many of my students and clients, friends, and family members over the last decade have confronted me repeatedly with my own need to grow. In responding to this confrontation I have learned some things about myself, especially about my resistance to growth. I've learned that it's much easier for me to talk and write about growth than to grow. In this awareness I'm challenged by the words of Rabindranath Tagore:

> A teacher can never truly teach unless he is still learning himself. A lamp can never light another lamp unless it continues to burn its own flame. The teacher . . . who has no living

traffic with his knowledge but merely repeats his lessons to his students can only lead their minds; he cannot quicken them.[1]

This truth about growth-enabling teaching also applies to any counseling or therapy that is to produce growth. The most difficult, yet potentially the most fulfilling aspect of being in a profession committed to growth is the fact that we can enable growth in others only to the degree that we are open, vulnerable, caring, risking, and growing ourselves.

So, to repeat for emphasis a point made in chapter 2, the place to begin, in enhancing your professional effectiveness, is with your own growth. By attending to your need for continuing growth you strengthen the primary source of increased effectiveness as a facilitator of growth for others. As growth enablers, we give our clients and students gifts (whether they recognize them as that or not) when we confront them honestly and caringly with the ways they are putting themselves down, selling themselves short, sabotaging their full effectiveness in living, neglecting the development of so many of their potentials. Perhaps we all need to give ourselves such a gift by confronting ourselves in a caring-loving way with how much more our lives could be.

I hope that what you have read in these pages has awakened feelings of zest about some unused possibilities in your own life. I hope that you now feel the lure of some things you *can* do and *want* to do to make your life more creative, fulfilling, and significant to others. The value to you of reading this book will be increased tremendously if you choose to respond in concrete ways to the lure of your own becoming.

Developing more of our gifts, as suggested earlier, involves using the principle of creative intentionality. I like Dorothy Jongward's and Dru Scott's description, in *Women as Winners*, of how this process can begin: "Deciding on growth means getting in touch with what is really important to you. What do you really value? Once you have a fix on this, you can make contracts for change. . . . Know what it is that you value enough to put your energies into making it happen."[2]

I suggest that you use the following growth exercise to move ahead in your personal-professional development. Using such an intentional process can help you firm up your own growth plans and equip you to coach clients and students in their uses of similar self-growth methods. As you will discover, the process that such an exercise begins can become an ongoing one:

Go back and review the insights and methods you have encountered in this book. Focus on those that caught your interest because you sensed their relevance to your personal growth or your work. Review the things you have underlined in the book and the insights that you have jotted in the margins or in your growth journal as you read. / Now, take time to relate some of these ideas and insights to your hopes and dreams for your own growth, personally and professionally, and to the growth needs of your institution and community. /

As an experiment, picture yourself the way you'd really like to be using more of your strengths and creativity. Close your eyes and *be* that growing, exciting person for several minutes. Let yourself experience the energy of that lively image of yourself. / Stay with this experience and become aware of some specific changes in yourself that will allow you to move toward becoming the person you imaged. Focus on the particular differences in yourself that you care about intensely enough to invest the time and energy it will probably require to actualize them. Perhaps you'd like to take better care of your body; learn to meditate; become more open and aware in close relationships; laugh more and have more fun; learn particular growth-enabling skills; write a poem, an article, or a book; acquire a certain professional credential or position; discover ways to contribute more to your field; get involved with others in helping to solve a growth-blocking social problem about which you have a strong concern.

List in your journal the growth directions or objectives that seem important to you. Write down only the goals of change that are energized for you–the directions toward which you feel pulled strongly. Now, decide on one or two of these personal or professional growth objectives that seem particularly important. / Let your mind play with these possibilities. Surround your growth directions with energy from your higher Self. Visualize yourself developing in these ways. Let yourself feel your power to change and the joy that can come from such growth. /

Staying with this experience, step by step, for moving in these directions, including a tentative schedule for taking the first crucial steps. It may help to develop your plans for your personal and your professional growth in parallel columns to see both the interrelatedness and the distinctiveness of these two dimensions. Decide what workshops, courses, training events, or therapy you need in order to move toward your personal and professional growth goals. Plan when and how you will have these experiences. /

Now, write out an agreement with yourself, a contract, spelling out concretely what you agree to do to develop the particular possibilities you have chosen. / Find several people who care about you and who are also growing. Contract with them to become a growth-support group, to encourage one another in the struggles and to celebrate together the satisfactions of growth. Check your growth objectives and your concrete plans with them to get their feedback. Such a growth-support group is worth whatever effort it takes to bring it into being. / In the months ahead, let further growth plans and contracts with yourself develop around your other important growth objectives. /

If you have discovered that this particular exercise isn't useful for you, I hope that you'll modify it or scrap it and develop your own approach that works for you. The most important thing, in all this, is to devise and implement an intentional plan that translates your growth needs and dreams into concrete actions, a plan that lets the tender new sprouts of your personal and professional becoming emerge and be nurtured.

Think of your growth now in the wider context of the wholeness needs of others–your friends, family, clients, and the needs of your community and world. Be aware of how your growth can enable you to respond more creatively and effectively to the wholeness needs of others.

The present moment in history is pregnant with unprecedented possibilities–for chaos or creativity, for alienation or community, for disintegration or growth. We may well be on the verge of a new stage in the human journey. In the midst of the epidemic of growth-stifling problems and injustices, the growth élan seems to be moving powerfully in many people and in many places. More and more people are, like you, beginning to feel the warm winds of spring awakening them to new growth in their bodies and minds, and in their relations with other people, nature, institutions, and with the birthing Spirit. The time is ripe for a fresh commitment, by all of us who are aware of the wonder-full potentials of human beings, to doing all that we can to help develop greater wholeness in ourselves, in our intimate relationships, in our community and its institutions, and among the whole human family. By sharing wholeheartedly in such a commitment, you may become an increasingly able "gardener of the Spirit" who will help make the darkness a time of birth and the light a time for wholeness to flower. Shalom!

Notes

CHAPTER 1

1. Herbert A. Otto estimates that most human beings function at 10 percent or less of their potential. See Otto, ed., *Human Potentialities: The Challenge and the Promise* (St. Louis: Warren H. Green, 1968), p. 3.

2. This list is adapted from Abraham Maslow's description of characteristics of a growing person in *Toward a Psychology of Being*, 2nd ed. (New York: Van Nostrand, 1968), p. 26.

3. Vasiti Davydor, "Inexhaustible Brain Potential," in *U.S.S.R.: Soviet Life Today* (November, 1964), pp. 42-45.

4. See Marjorie Fiske Lowenthal and Clayton Haven, "Interaction and Adaptation: Intimacy as a Crucial Variable," *American Sociological Review*, vol. 33 (1968), pp. 20-30.

5. E. Mansell Pattison, *Pastor and Parish–A Systems Approach* (Philadelphia: Fortress Press, 1977), p. 19.

6. D. H. Lawrence, *Poems*, Vol. III (London: William Heinemann, 1939), p. 529.

7. See Clinebell, *Well Being, A Personal Plan for Exploring and Enriching the Seven Dimensions of Life* (San Francisco: Harper San Francisco, 1992), pp. 118-122.

8. Cited by Howard Stone, in *Crisis Counseling* (Philadelphia: Fortress Press, 1976), p. 3.

9. See Harvey Seifert and Clinebell, *Personal Growth and Social Change* (Philadelphia: Westminster Press, 1969), pp. 19-22.

10. David C. McClelland explores these issues illuminatingly in *Power: The Inner Experience* (New York: Wiley, 1975).

11. Rollo May, *Power and Innocence* (New York: Wiley, 1975).

12. See Clinebell, "Religion and Creative Social Change," in *Cultures in Collision*, Issy Pilowsky, ed. (Australian Association for Mental Health, 1975). See also Dorothy Day's biography, *The Long Loneliness* (New York: Harper, 1952).

13. Jessie Bernard, *The Future of Marriage* (New York: Bantam Books, 1972), chap. 2; Judith Laws, "A Feminist View of Marital Adjustment," in *Couples in Conflict: New Directions in Marital Therapy*, Alan S. Gurman and Daniel G. Rice, eds. (New York: Jason Aronson, 1975), chap. 3.

14. See Myron Brenton, *The American Male* (New York: Coward, McCann & Geoghegan, 1966); Herb Goldberg, *The Hazards of Being Male* (New York: New American Library, 1976); Marc F. Fasteau, *The Male Machine* (New York:

McGraw-Hill, 1974); and William L. Malcomson, *Success Is a Failure Experience* (Nashville: Abingdon, 1976).

15. For an in-depth discussion of these issues see, "Challenges to Your Well Being as a Woman or Man–Creative Coping", Clinebell, *Well Being*, pp. 257-276.

16. I am indebted to my friend John Cobb for this illustration.

CHAPTER 2

1. Duane Elgin, "What Waits Beyond America's Newest Frontier?" *Los Angeles Times* (December 19, 1974).

2. Abraham Maslow, *Toward a Psychology of Being*, 2nd ed. (New York: Van Nostrand, 1968), p. 25.

3. This insight is from John Cobb, *Theology and Pastoral Care* (Philadelphia: Fortress Press, 1977), p. 52.

4. Ezra Stotland, *The Psychology of Hope* (San Francisco: Jossey-Bass, 1969), pp. 21-22.

5. The original was quoted by Willard Gaylin in "Caring Makes the Difference," *Psychology Today* (August, 1976), p. 39.

6. Rollo May, *Love and Will* (New York: W. W. Norton, 1969), pp. 218, 223-24.

7. Robert Rosenthal, "The Pygmalion Effect Lives," *Psychology Today* (September, 1973), p. 58; "On the Social Psychology of the Self-Fulfilling Prophecy: Further Evidence for Pygmalion Effects and Their Mediating Mechanisms" (New York: MSS Modular Publications, 1973).

8. A constructive use of the concept "original sin" is discussed in *The Mental Health Ministry of the Local Church*, p. 40 n. 16. I am aware that, when seen in the context of the gospel, the concept of original sin need not foster hopelessness or resignation.

9. Maslow, *Toward a Psychology of Being*, p. vii.

10. Theodore Roszak, *The Unfinished Animal* (New York: Harper, 1975), p. 251.

11. See Clinebell, *Basic Types of Pastoral Care and Counseling*, (Nashville: Abingdon Press, 1984, Rev. Ed.), pp. 349-372.

12. For a competent pastoral psychotherapist, contact the American Association of Pastoral Counselors, 9504 A Lee Highway, Fairfax, VA 22031; phone: (703) 385-6967; FAX: (703) 352-7725.

13. Jean Baker Miller, "Psychoanalysis, Patriarchy, and Power," *Chrysalis* (Summer, 1977), pp. 19-25.

14. See Henri J. M. Nouwen. *The Wounded Healer* (New York: Doubleday, 1972).

15. Adapted from Clinebell, *Growth Counseling for Marriage Enrichment*, pp. 29-30.

CHAPTER 3

1. For a full description of this awareness exercise, see Clinebell, *Well Being*, pp. 289-292.

2. For more complete instructions on revising a marital contract, see Clinebell, *Well Being*, pp. 122-126.

3. For a description of other methods of sexual enrichment, see *Well Being*, "Sex and Well Being," chapter 10.

CHAPTER 4

1. For an in-depth discussion of the spiritual center of humanness see: "Enriching and Enjoying Your Spiritual Life–Wellspring of Love, Well Being, and Joy," *Well Being*, chapter 2.

2. Erich Fromm, *Psychoanalysis and Religion* (New Haven: Yale University Press, 1950), pp. 24-25.

3. For a more in-depth discussion of healing pathogenic and facilitating salugenic religion see Clinebell, *Basic Types of Pastoral Care and Counseling* (Nashville: Abingdon Press, 1984), chapter 5.

4. For a discussion of this view see Clinebell, *Understanding and Counseling the Alcoholic* (Nashville: Abingdon, 1968), chap. 6.

5. Anne Kent Rush, *Getting Clear: Body Work for Women* (New York: Random House, 1973), p. 281.

6. Carlos Castaneda, *Journey to Ixtlan* (New York: Simon & Schuster, 1973), p. 55; Elisabeth Kübler-Ross, *Death: The Final Stage of Growth* (Englewood Cliffs, N.J.: Prentice-Hall, 1975), pp. 164-165.

7. Bynner Witter, *The Way of Life According to Lao Tsu* (New York: Capricorn Books, 1962), p. 71.

8. "Talking with Jack Harris," Albans Institute Action Information (June, 1976), p. 6.

9. Robert J. Lifton, *The Life of the Self* (New York: Simon & Schuster, 1976), p. 135.

10. A survey reported in the *Los Angeles Times* (February 28, 1977), p. 6, revealed that 12 percent of a cross-section sample of Americans said that they are involved in some type of mystical discipline. Forty-four percent said that they have had a "genuine mystical experience" during their lives. This trend continues today.

11. Mary Daly, *Beyond God the Father* (Boston: Beacon Press, 1973), p. 28.

12. Abraham Maslow, *The Farther Reaches of Human Nature* (New York: Viking Press, 1971), p. 325.

13. See Jean Baker Miller, *Toward a New Psychology of Women* (Boston: Beacon Press, 1976).

14. See Clinebell, "Counseling on Ethical, Value, and Meaning Issues," *Basic Types of Pastoral Care and Counseling*, chapter 6.

15. Roberto Assagioli, *Psychosynthesis* (New York: Viking Press, 1971), p. 314.

16. Herbert Benson, *Relaxation Response* (New York: Morrow, 1975), see pp. 70-71, for a summary of these findings.

17. Lawrence LeShan, *How to Meditate* (New York: Bantam Books, 1974); Morton T. Kelsey, *The Other Side of Silence* (New York: Paulist Press, 1976); William Johnson, *Silent Music: The Science of Meditation* (New York: Harper, 1974); Carolyn Stahl, *Opening to God* (Nashville: The Upper Room, 1977).

18. Witter, *The Way of Life According to Lao Tsu*, p. 42.

19. Pierre Teilhard de Chardin, *The Divine Milieu* (New York: Harper, 1965), p. 60.

20. See Maslow, *The Farther Reaches*, p. 105.

21. James Fadman and Robert Frager, *Personality and Growth* (New York: Harper, 1976), pp. 347-348.

22. Edward K. Perry, "Learning About Fishing in Upper New York" (Syracuse, N.Y.: The Upper New York Synod of the Lutheran Church in America, 1978).

23. Robert Gerard, "Evolution of Consciousness," Integral Psychology Monographs (1972), pp. 13-14.

CHAPTER 5

1. Conceptions of healing and wholeness differ widely among various religious traditions; many of these contrast sharply with understandings from contemporary psychotherapies.

2. John Calvin, *Commentaries on the First Book of Moses Called Genesis*, vol. 1, trans. John King (Grand Rapids: Eerdmans, 1948), p. 96.

3. See Gerhard van Rad, *Genesis: A Commentary*, trans. John H. Marks (Philadelphia: Westminster Press, 1961), p. 56.

4. See John B. Cobb, Jr., and David R. Griffin, *Process Theology* (Philadelphia: Westminster Press, 1976), chap. 3.

5. See Cobb, *Theology and Pastoral Care* (Philadelphia: Fortress Press, 1977), chap. 3.

6. I am indebted to feminist theologian, the late Nelle Morton for this insight.

7. Paul Tillich, *Systematic Theology*, vol. 3, part 1 (Chicago: University of Chicago Press, 1951), pp. 228-243.

8. Elisabeth Schussler Fiorenza, "Feminist Theology as a Critical Theology of Liberation," *Theological Studies*, vol. 36 (December, 1975), p. 625. The encounter of Mary Magdala and the other women with Jesus liberated their lives profoundly, as did the encounters of men with him.

9. See Douglas J. Harris, *The Biblical Concept of Peace, Shalom* (Grand Rapids: Baker Book House, 1970).

10. Corita Kent and Joseph Pintauró, *To Believe in God* (New York: Harper, 1968).

11. See Don Browning, "Rogers, Perls and Schutz in Theological and Philosophical Perspective," *Dialogue: A Journal of Theology*, vol. 13 (Spring, 1974), pp. 104-9.

12. Schubert Ogden, *The Reality of God* (New York: Harper, 1963), p. 216.

13. See John Macquarrie, "The Struggle of Conscience for Authentic Self-hood," *Conscience Theological and Psychological Perspectives*, E. Ellis, ed. (New York: Newman Press, 1973), p. 158.

14. Nelle Morton, "Toward a Whole Theology," *Lutheran World* (January, 1975), p. 14.

15. See Rosemary Radford Ruether, *New Woman New Earth* (New York: The Seabury Press, 1975), and Mary Daly, *Beyond God the Father* (Boston: Beacon Press, 1973), for full documentation of this alliance.

16. Sarah Josepha Hale, *Woman's Record ... From the Creation to A.D. 1854.* (New York: Harper, 1855), p. xxxvi. She also pointed out that the "help" Adam needed and Eve was equipped to give him was in those higher spiritual qualities in which he was deficient. I am indebted to Sharleen Martenas for calling my attention to the work of these women scholars.

17. Fiorenza, "Feminist Theology as a Critical Theology of Liberation," p. 617.

18. Phylis Trible, *God and the Rhetoric of Sexuality* (Philadelphia: Fortress Press, 1978), p. 202.

19. See Leonard Swidler, "Jesus Was a Feminist," *Catholic World* (January, 1971).

20. Nelle Morton, *The Journey Is Home* (Boston, Beacon Press, 1985); Plant and Christ, *Weaving the Visions* (San Francisco: Harper and Row, 1985); Clare Benedicks Fischer et al., eds. *Women in a Strange Land* (Philadelphia: Fortress Press, 1975); Merlin Store, *When God Was a Woman* (New York: Dial Press, 1976).

21. Morton, "The Rising Woman Consciousness in a Male Language Structure," p. 190.

22. Personal communication with Morton.

23. Morton, "Hearing to Speech" (sermon at the School of Theology at Claremont, April 27, 1977), p. 2. She points out that John Macquarrie observes that *wind* and *fire* are synonymous with the Hebrew word for "spirit" and that all three words are feminine images.

24. See Carol P. Christ, "Why Women Need the Goddess" (paper presented at the 1977 American Academy of Religion meeting), p. 6.

25. The dominant expression of human spirituality in the Near East and elsewhere, for many centuries before the Old Testament began to take shape, centered on the veneration of the feminine in divinity—the great Goddess (who was called by many different names). Far from being worshiped mainly as a fertility symbol, as I was taught in Old Testament courses in seminary, she was revered in many cultures as the creator and sustainer of life, the source of wisdom, law, and the arts. In ancient Crete, where the feminine in divinity was at the center of the culture, women probably were esteemed and took part in public life and social leadership in ways that were largely denied them in subsequent patriarchal times, in-

cluding the present. After the takeover by patriarchal religious leaders, the great Goddess was depicted as a depraved fertility deity and the male gods were described as the source of wisdom, justice, and right. See Merlin Stone, for a full discussion of this ancient heritage.

26. Morton, "A Word We Cannot Yet Speak," pp. 22-23.

CHAPTER 6

1. Here is Erik Erikson's description of the epigenetic principle: "Whenever we try to understand growth, it is well to remember the epigenetic principle which is derived from the growth of organisms in utero. . . . This principle states that anything that grows has a ground plan, and that out of that ground plan the parts arise, each part having its time of special ascendency. . . . Personality . . . can be said to develop according to steps predetermined in the organism's readiness to be driven forward, to be aware of, and to interact with a widening radius of significant individuals and institutions," *Identity, Youth and Crisis* (New York: W. W. Norton, 1968), pp. 92-93.

2. Don Browning, *Generative Man* (Philadelphia: Westminster Press, 1973), p. 181.

3. Ibid., p. 162.

4. Erikson, *Identity, Youth and Crisis*, p. 96.

5. Erikson, *Childhood and Society* (New York: W. W. Norton, 1963), p. 413.

6. See Kate Millet, *Sexual Politics* (New York: Doubleday, 1969), pp. 210-221; Erikson, "Inner and Outer Space: Reflections on Womanhood," *Daedalus* 93 (1964), pp. 582-606.

7. Ann B. Ulanov, "The Place of Religion in the Training of Pastoral Counselors," *Journal of Religion and Health*, vol. 15 (1976), p. 79.

8. Erikson, *Young Man Luther* (New York: W. W. Norton, 1958); Erikson, *Gandhi's Truth* (New York: W. W. Norton, 1969).

9. See "Moral Development," *The International Encyclopedia of the Social Sciences* (New York: Crowell, Collier, MacMillan, 1968), pp. 483-89.

10. LeRoy Aden, "Faith and the Developmental Cycle," *Pastoral Psychology*, vol. 24 (Spring, 1976); John J. Gleason, Jr., *Growing Up to God: 8 Steps in Religious Development* (Nashville: Abingdon, 1975); James W. Fowler, III, "Toward a Developmental Perspective on Faith," *Religious Education*, vol. 13 (March-April, 1974).

11. Aden, "Faith and the Developmental Cycle," p. 215.

12. Jean Baker Miller, ed., *Psychoanalysis and Women* (New York: Brunner/Mazel, 1973), p. 396.

13. Erikson, *Insight and Responsibility* (New York: W. W. Norton, 1964), pp. 115, 118.

14. Erikson, "On the Sense of Inner Identity," *Psychoanalytic Psychiatry and Psychology*, vol. 1, Robert Knight and Cyrus R. Friedman, eds. (New York: International Universities Press, 1954), p. 353.

15. Adrienne Rich, *Of Woman Born: Motherhood as Experience and Institution* (New York: Bantam Books, 1977), p. xv.

16. Ibid.; Dorothy Dinnerstern, *The Mermaid and the Minotaur, Sexual Arrangements and Human Malaise* (New York: Harper Colophon Books, 1976).

17. Miller, *Psychoanalysis and Women*, p. 394.

18. See Clinebell, *Growth Groups*, chap. 7.

19. See Carrie Carmichael, *Non-Sexist Childraising* (Boston: Beacon Press, 1977).

20. See Clinebell, *Growth Groups*, chap. 6.

21. Judith M. Bordwick and Elizabeth Douvan, "Ambivalence: The Socialization of Women," *Women in a Sexist Society*, Vivian Gornick and Berhara K. Morgan eds. (New York: New American Library, 1972), pp. 232-233, 238.

22. Reesa M. Vaughter, "Psychology," *Signs: Journal of Women in Culture and Society*, vol. 2 (Autumn, 1976), p. 127.

23. Roger L. Gould, "The Phases of Adult Life: A Study in Developmental Psychology," *American Journal of Psychiatry* (November, 1972), 129:5.

24. For a discussion of how such programs can be set up in a church see Clinebell, *Growth Counseling for Marriage Enrichment*, chap. 6.

25. Erikson, *Gandhi's Truth*, p. 395.

26. Gould, "The Phases of Adult Life," p. 523.

27. Beatrice Neugarten et al., *Personality in Middle and Late Life* (New York: Atherton Press, 1964), p. 198.

28. See Clinebell, *Growth Counseling for Mid-Years Couples*.

29. Miller, *Psychoanalysis and Women*, p. 396.

30. See Naomi R. Goldenberg, "Feminist Witchcraft–The Goddess is Alive" (paper) (University of Ottawa, 1977), pp. 18-20.

31. See Clinebell, *Growth Counseling for Mid-Years Couples*, pp. 50-58.

32. For further resources on bereavement and grief groups see Clinebell, "Bereavement Care and Counseling," *Basic Types of Pastoral Care and Counseling*; chapter 9. Also two video series are available–see "Healing Your Grief Wound, A New Resource for the Grieving" and "Growing Through Grief: Personal Healing" in the annotated bibliography.

33. Eugene O'Neill, *Ah, Wilderness and Two Other Plays* (New York: Modern Library, 1964), p. 141.

34. Elisabeth Kübler-Ross, *Death: The Final Stage of Growth*, pp. 79-80.

35. Erikson, *Insight and Responsibility*, p. 115.

SUMMARY AND CONCLUSION

1. *World Education Reports*, no. 16 (March, 1978), cover.

2. Dorothy Jongward and Dru Scott, *Women as Winners: Transactional Analysis for Personal Growth* (Reading, Mass.: Addison-Wesley, 1976), p. 293.

Bibliography

For Further Exploration
of Growth Counseling

Aronoff, Joel. *Psychological Needs and Cultural System* (New York: Van Nostrand, 1976). Uses Maslow's theory of personality to develop a conception of the relation between basic psychological needs and cultural institutions.

Clinebell, Charlotte H. *Counseling for Liberation* (Philadelphia: Fortress Press, 1976). Explores counseling and consciousness-raising as methods of liberating women-men relationships.

Clinebell, Howard. *Basic Types of Pastoral Counseling* (Nashville: Abingdon, 1984). Discusses the theory and methodologies of the major types of counseling from a holistic, growth-oriented perspective.

_____ . *Contemporary Growth Therapies: Resources for Actualizing Human Wholeness* (Nashville: Abingdon, 1981). Describes insights and methods for facilitating growth from some twenty-five psychotherapies.

_____ . *Growing Through Grief: Personal Healing* (Nashville, EcuFilm, 1984). Six video programs with a users guide; shows a grief healing group led by Howard Clinebell, who comments on what is occurring and shares insights about the topics. Useful in grief groups.

_____ . *Healing Your Grief Wound, A New Resource for the Grieving* (Well Being, Inc., 780 W. 9th, Claremont, CA 91711). A two part video series designed to help bereaved persons. The first tape deals with handling the grim early weeks after a painful loss; the second deals with grief issues during the first year following such a loss.

_____ . *Nurtured by Nature/Nuturing Nature: A Guide to Ecologi-*

cally Grounded Personality Theory, Ecotherapy and Ecoeducation (Minneapolis, MN: Fortress Press, forthcoming). Therapeutic earthcaring for psychotherapists, pastoral counselors, teachers, mental and physical health professionals, and parents.

_____ . *Well Being, A Personal Plan for Exploring and Enriching the Seven Dimensions of Life: Mind, Body, Spirit, Love, Work, Play, Earth* (San Francisco: Harper San Francisco, 1992). A do-it-yourself workbook containing many methods for enhancing self-care-for-wellness in the seven dimensions, as well as in crises and losses, sexuality, women and men health issue, and well being through the life stages. A series of five Well Being videotapes parallels chapters in the book, and a guide for using the book and videos in congregations is available. (Well Being, Inc., 780 W. 9th, Claremont, CA 91711.)

_____ . *Understanding and Counseling the Alcoholic, Through Psychology and Religion* (Nashville: Abingdon, Revised Edition forthcoming). A guide to understanding various religious approaches to alcoholism including AA, and for counseling with addicted persons and their families.

_____ . *Growth Counseling for Marriage Enrichment, Pre-Marriage and the Early Years* (Philadelphia: Fortress Press, 1975). Applies the growth counseling approach to marriage enrichment, particularly during the preparation and early stages.

_____ . *Growth Counseling for Mid-Years Couples* (Philadelphia: Fortress Press, 1977). Marriage enrichment and counseling methods for the mid years.

_____ . *Growth Groups* (Nashville: Abingdon, 1977). Spells out the growth-group approach and applies it to marriage and family enrichment, creative singlehood, youth work, women's and men's liberation, social problems.

Erikson, Erik. *The Life Cycle Completed* (New York: W.W. Norton, 1982). A retrospective overview of the eight stages of the life cycle from a historical and autobiographical perspective.

Gould, Roger L. *Transformations, Growth and Change in Adult Life* (New York: Simon & Schuster, 1978). Describes growthful ways of coping with adult life crises.

Maslow, Abraham H. *The Farther Reaches of Human Nature* (New York: Viking Press, 1971). Explores health and pathology, creativeness, values, education, transcendence, and "metamotivation."

_____ . *Religions, Values and Peak Experiences* (Columbus: Ohio State University Press, 1964). Discusses transcendental experiences, the split between science and religion, hope and values in education.

_____ . *Toward a Psychology of Being*, 2d ed. (New York: Van Nostrand, 1968). A classic statement of Maslow's growth-oriented psychology.

Miller, Jean Baker. *Toward a New Psychology of Women* (Boston: Beacon Press, 1976). Describes how growth is stifled by sexism and how it can be liberated.

Otto, Herbert A., ed. *Human Potentialities: The Challenge and the Promise* (St. Louis: Warren H. Green, 1968). A collection of papers by Gardner Murphy, Abraham Maslow, Charlotte Buhler, Clark Moustakas, Alexander Lowen, Herbert Otto, and others exploring human potentials.

Schultz, Duane. *Growth Psychology: Models of Healthy Personality* (New York: Van Nostrand, 1977). Discusses the nature of wholeness in the thought of Allport, Rogers, Fromm, Maslow, Jung, Frankl, and Perls.

Shostrom, Everett L. *Actualizing Therapy* (San Diego: Edits Publishers, 1976). A synthesis of growth concepts and methods from various psychotherapeutic approaches.

Stotland, Ezra. *The Psychology of Hope* (San Francisco: Jossey-Bass, 1968). Discusses the relation of hope to anxiety, action, other people, psychosis, and therapy in the research literature.

Swimme, Brian and Berry, Thomas, *The Universe Story, From the Primordial Flaring Forth to the Ecozoic Era* (San Francisco: Harper San Francisco, 1992). A new creation story based on scientific knowledge about the unfolding of the cosmos, and the place of humans in this story.

Index